Reformation of Renfrewshire

1830–1872

Professor Samina Sultana, Ph.D.

© Copyright 2024 by BengalGeek™ - All rights reserved.

Published by BengalGeek™ LLC: www.bengalgeek.com

The content contained within this book may not be reproduced, duplicated or transmitted without direct written permission from the author or the publisher.

Under no circumstances will any blame or legal responsibility be held against the publisher, or author, for any damages, reparation, or monetary loss due to the information contained within this book, either directly or indirectly.

Legal Notice:

This book is copyright protected. It is only for personal use. You cannot amend, distribute, sell, use, quote or paraphrase any part, or the content within this book, without the consent of the author or publisher.

Disclaimer Notice:

Please note the information contained within this document is for educational and entertainment purposes only. All effort has been executed to present accurate, up to date, reliable, complete information. No warranties of any kind are declared or implied. Readers acknowledge that the author is not engaged in the rendering of legal, financial, medical or professional advice. The content within this book has been derived from various sources. Please consult a licensed professional before attempting any techniques outlined in this book.

By reading this document, the reader agrees that under no circumstances is the author responsible for any losses, direct or indirect, that are incurred as a result of the use of the information contained within this document, including, but not limited to, errors, omissions, or inaccuracies.

Dedicated to

Professor Ainun Nishat, PhD.

Contents

........◆........

FOREWARD x
ABSTRACT xiii
ABBREVIATIONS xv
PREFACE xvii

Chapter 1: Geographical, Social and Economic Background ...1
   1.1 Introduction 1
      Geographical Features 1
   1.2 Population Growth 2
      Social and Economic Background 2
   1.3 Industrial and Occupational Structure in Renfrewshire 14
   1.4 Conclusion 29

Chapter 2: The Denominational Role in Education in Renfrewshire 31
   2.1 The Role of the Established Church in Education in Renfrewshire 31
      2.1.1 Introduction 31
   2.2 The Contribution of the Heritors Toward Education 44
   2.3 Conclusion 47

Chapter 3: Structure of Education: The Denominational Role in Education in Renfrewshire 48

3.1 The Role Played by the Free Church in Education in Renfrewshire 48

    3.1.1 The Free Church in Scotland and Renfrewshire 48

    3.1.2 The Contribution of the Free Church to Education in Scotland and Renfrewshire 51

3.2 The Role Played by the Catholic Church in Education 60

    3.2.1 Introduction 60

    3.2.2 The Efforts of the Catholics for Education in Scotland and Renfrewshire 62

3.3 The Role Played by the Episcopal Church in Education 71

3.4 Conclusion 75

Chapter 4: The Secular Efforts in Education in Renfrewshire 77

4.1 The Role of the State 77

4.2 The Contribution of the Town Councils 83

    4.2.1 Burgh Schools in Scotland and Renfrewshire 83

    4.2.2 Power and Duties of the Council 85

    4.2.3 Role Played by the Burgh Schools in Renfrewshire 87

4.3 Subscription Schools (Infant, Endowed, Industrial and Factory) 93

    4.3.1 Introduction 93

    4.3.2 Infant and Endowed Schools 94

    4.3.3 Industrial and Ragged School 96

    4.3.4 Factory Schools 100

    4.3.5 Standard of Education in Subscription Schools 102

4.4 Private Adventure Schools 107

    4.4.1 Adventure Schools in Scotland and Renfrewshire 107

  4.4.2 Number of adventure schools and scholars in Renfrewshire 110

 4.5 Conclusion 114

Chapter 5: Quality of Educational Facilities 118

 5.1 Qualification of Teachers in Different Schools 118

 5.2 Pupil-Teacher Ratio 125

 5.3 Curriculum 128

 5.4 Discipline and School Life 132

 5.5 The Quality of School Buildings 134

 5.6 Availability of Equipment in the Schools 138

 5.7 Conclusion 139

Chapter 6: Regional Variations in Attendance 141

 6.1 Introduction 141

 6.2 Child Labor 141

 6.3 Population Expansion and Economic Depression Causing Regional Variation Absences 147

 6.4 Conclusion 155

Chapter 7: Conclusion 157

Bibliography 162

Appendix 174

Endnotes 178

FOREWARD

......◆......

I am delighted to share a remarkable piece of work - a book penned by my mother during her MPhil program at the University of Strathclyde, Glasgow. While supporting my father in his Ph.D. program, my mother devoted herself to researching and writing with the guidance of her professors, Professor Butt and Professor Hamnet. The outcome of her hard work is a highly engaging and informative book that is sure to captivate any reader. My mother was the only female student during her studies and wore a saree, a testament to her dedication and perseverance. Furthermore, her professor, Dr. Butt, went above and beyond by visiting my parents in Bangladesh, forging a lasting friendship. I am confident that my mother's impressive achievements will inspire anyone who reads this book.

This compelling book explores the transformation of education in Renfrewshire, Scotland, from 1830 to 1872. It provides fascinating details about the educational reformation of this small Scottish town and helps readers understand its impact on the community.

The manuscript has undergone rigorous editing, including spelling checks and rewriting while preserving the original work's essence. I, one of my son's friends, along with Darby Barrow and Mallory Wiper's professional editing assistance, have ensured that the book meets the highest standards of American English specifications.

We have intentionally preserved some spelling discrepancies to maintain the authentic associations, and other entities are presented as they are officially named. This book has been a great source of education and inspiration for us, and we believe it will be for you, too. If you have any questions or concerns or want to explore other publications, please do not hesitate to contact me at www.bengalgeek.com.

—*Uzma Nishat*

Samina Sultana and her husband, Ainun Nishat, in Glasgow, UK in 1979

ABSTRACT

........◆........

Renfrewshire experienced economic and social changes from industrialization in the west of Scotland. Urbanization and migration that accompanied industrialization made the county one of Scotland's most densely populated areas. This social and economic change, in turn, greatly impacted education. This study examines the structure of education in Renfrewshire between 1830 and 1872.

Chapter One provides an overview of the period's social and economic background, including information on the population expansion and different industries that emerged and declined. It also discusses the occupational structure and wages of people during this time.

Chapter Two focuses on the Established Church and the heritors, exploring whether they could meet the needs of the growing population. Chapter Three continues this discussion, examining the contributions of other churches, such as Free, Catholic, and Episcopal, and whether they could increase the number of school places available.

Chapter Four examines the state's increasing involvement in education, including government inspection and grants. It also covers the efforts of town councils and the importance of subscription and adventure schools in response to the growing population.

Chapter Five examines the quality of educational facilities, such as teacher training, the pupil-teacher ratio, the curriculum, and the availability of equipment and school buildings.

Finally, Chapter Six assesses regional differences in attendance, considering factors such as child labor and the presence of migrant groups. Throughout the book, comparisons are made with other countries where applicable.

Research has revealed the pressures that strained the traditional educational structure. Although the number of school places in the parish and other schools run by the Church of Scotland increased—despite the church's decreasing influence in education—it was not enough to meet the educational demand.

After 1843, the Free Church established several schools. The Catholic church also tried to address its followers' educational needs. The state-supported these churches and other secular organizations with grants and inspections to meet the growing demand for education. Subscription and adventure schools were critical in educating the county's children, although the quality of education varied. Nearly half of the children in the area attended these schools. Unfortunately, it is difficult to determine whether there was an increase in the number of schools in the county due to a lack of information. However, it is believed that the number of students increased more than the population. Overall, the quality of education the different church schools provided was satisfactory, but the standard was relatively low in most adventure, some of the subscription, and Catholic schools.

The adverse effects of the economic changes are reflected in non-attendance in urban areas, especially among Catholic children, on account of child labor. Despite the Factory Legislation, many children still worked different jobs. In 1871, 35% of the children in the county aged 5–13 were not on any school roll. The study reveals that the education problem was similar in other lowland counties of Scotland.

ABBREVIATIONS

⋯⋯◆⋯⋯

ACI, II, and III:	Argyle Commission on Education in Scotland—First, Second, and Third Reports
ARPIS:	Annual Report, Paisley Industrial School
CCE:	Committee of the Privy Council on Education in Scotland
CCM:	Minutes and Reports 1839-1939
ECC:	Educational Committee of the Church of Scotland
ERC:	Education Committee, Report of the General Assembly of the Church of Scotland
ESHC:	Endowed Schools and Hospital (Scotland) Commission
FIR:	Factory Inspector's Report
HM:	Her Majesty's (Inspectors and Commissioners)
NSA:	New Statistical Accounts
PC:	Privy Council
PCIP:	Parliamentary Commission of the State of the Irish Poor in Great Britain

PGAF:	Proceedings of the General Assembly of the Free Church of Scotland
RCES:	Royal Commission on Education in Scotland
SCES:	Select Commission on Education in Scotland
TSA:	Third Statistical Accounts
UP:	United Presbytery

PREFACE

.... ♦ ....

Renfrewshire was one of the main areas of Scotland that underwent profound social change due to industrialization in the early nineteenth century. Population growth and industrialization contributed to industrial change, inevitably significantly affecting education.

This book aims to examine the structure of education in Renfrewshire in the middle decades of the nineteenth century and to assess the extent of change between the 1830s and the coming of a full-state elementary system in 1872. The study's limits stem from the sources, mainly parliamentary papers and census data. These were Parliamentary Returns of 1841, 1854, 1862, 1863, and 1867. In the 1841 return, there was information about the number of children in 1836–37, the number of teachers, subjects taught, fees, how the schools were inspected and examined, and similar topics. The primary deficiency was that there was no data about absenteeism, and 66 out of 177 schools did not answer the queries instituted by a Select Committee on Education in Scotland (S.C.E.S.). The 1867 Parliamentary Paper (Argyle Commission, 1st report) contained no information from Paisley, Greenock, and a portion on Abbey Parish, Paisley. The gap has been filled by details from 1854 and 1862 for Paisley, Greenock, and Abbey Paisley. These last two returns reveal the data about the schools under the religious bodies. They probably included burgh schools and missed some adventure and subscription schools in Abbey Paisley. None of these three returns included data on the absenteeism ratio, subjects followed, fees charged, or other related information. There is also detailed information about the burgh schools in the 1867 Assistant Commissioner's Report (Argyle Commission III Report). The Census of Scotland 1871 added information about the number of scholars out of the total number of children. The number of grants to different schools from the Committee of Council on Education (C.C.E.) was collected from the Parliamentary Papers of 1856/7, 1863, and so on, revealing the number of certificated teachers.

Given that the educational system in Scotland had grown mainly based on the Church of Scotland, a central question was how the church's position in education altered. In the nineteenth century, an element of the middle classes called for state control in education. Demands for secular education led to increased involvement of the state. With its grants and different educational legislations, the state became more involved in education than ever. The Church of Scotland's dominant position was also weakened by the Disruption of 1843. The Education Act of 1861 ultimately ended the connection between the Established Church and the parish schools, and eventually, the state took complete control in 1872.

As a result of the Disruption, the Free Church immediately built up an educational system to rival the parish schools. Another key feature of the 1840s was the development of Roman Catholic education in response to the massive migration of Irish people into Renfrewshire, especially in the aftermath of the Famine.

It is relatively apparent, however, that religious organizations were not offering enough educational opportunities of the right kind to meet the demands of a growing population in urban areas, and many alternatives to church schools were provided in subscription and adventure schools. In growing towns, there were attempts to deliver a higher level of education in secondary schools.

Forming any assessment of the quality of education offered in the different types of schools is challenging. Standards varied significantly based on the quality of the individual teachers. Nonetheless, some attempts are made to measure quality by examining what was being taught and the extent of qualifications among the teachers. Any conclusions in this area have to be very tentative.

This study aims to evaluate how the educational system in Renfrewshire changed during the 19th century due to the rapid industrialization, urbanization, and immigration that occurred. This resulted in a gradual shift of control from the church to the state. To understand whether the traditional structure was overwhelmed, examining the efforts of different denominational and secular bodies is crucial. The study will highlight if there was enough resilience in the system to prevent a complete collapse, and, if so, what the elements of that resilience were. Additionally, the study will compare the changes in Renfrewshire with other areas of Scotland, like Ayrshire and Stirlingshire, to determine if the changes were typical of an industrial county.

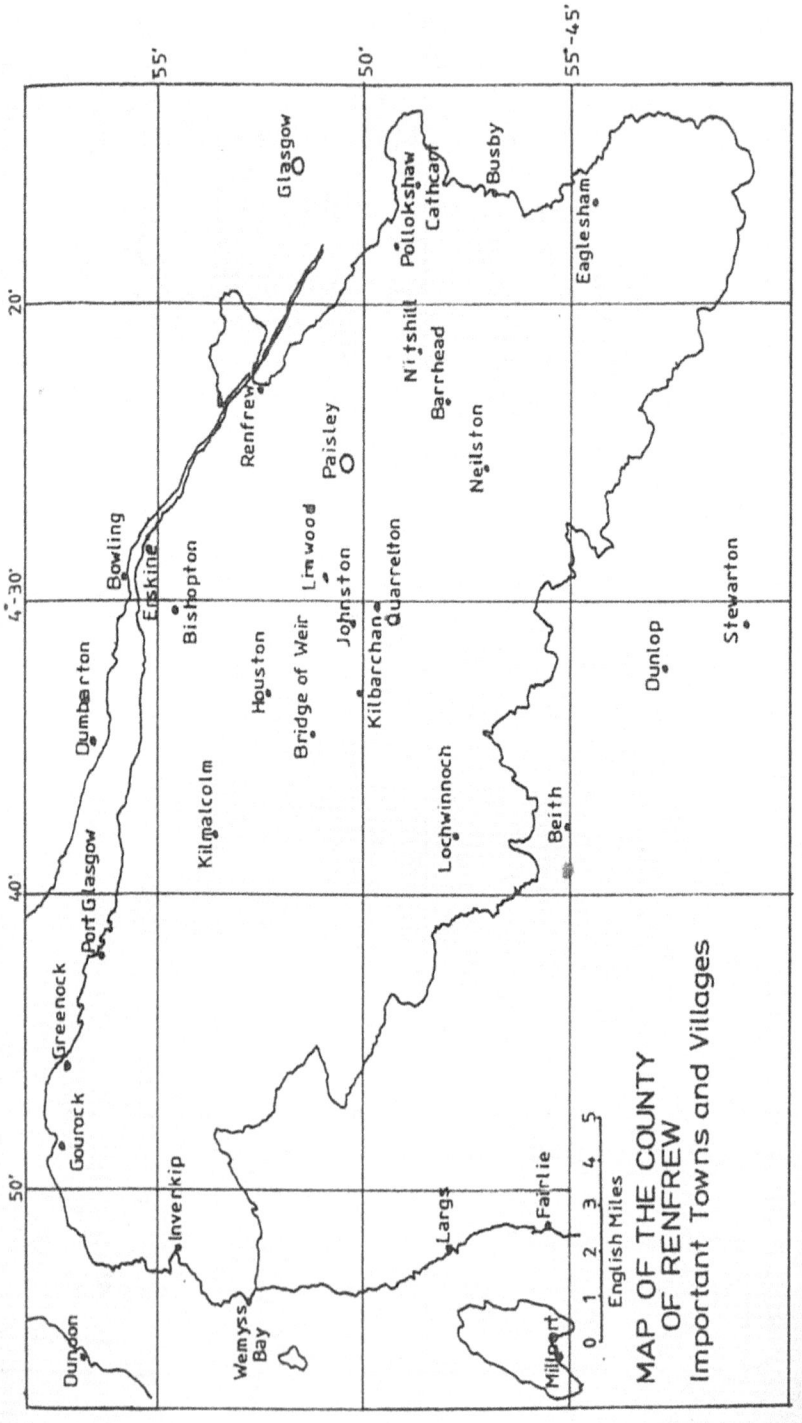

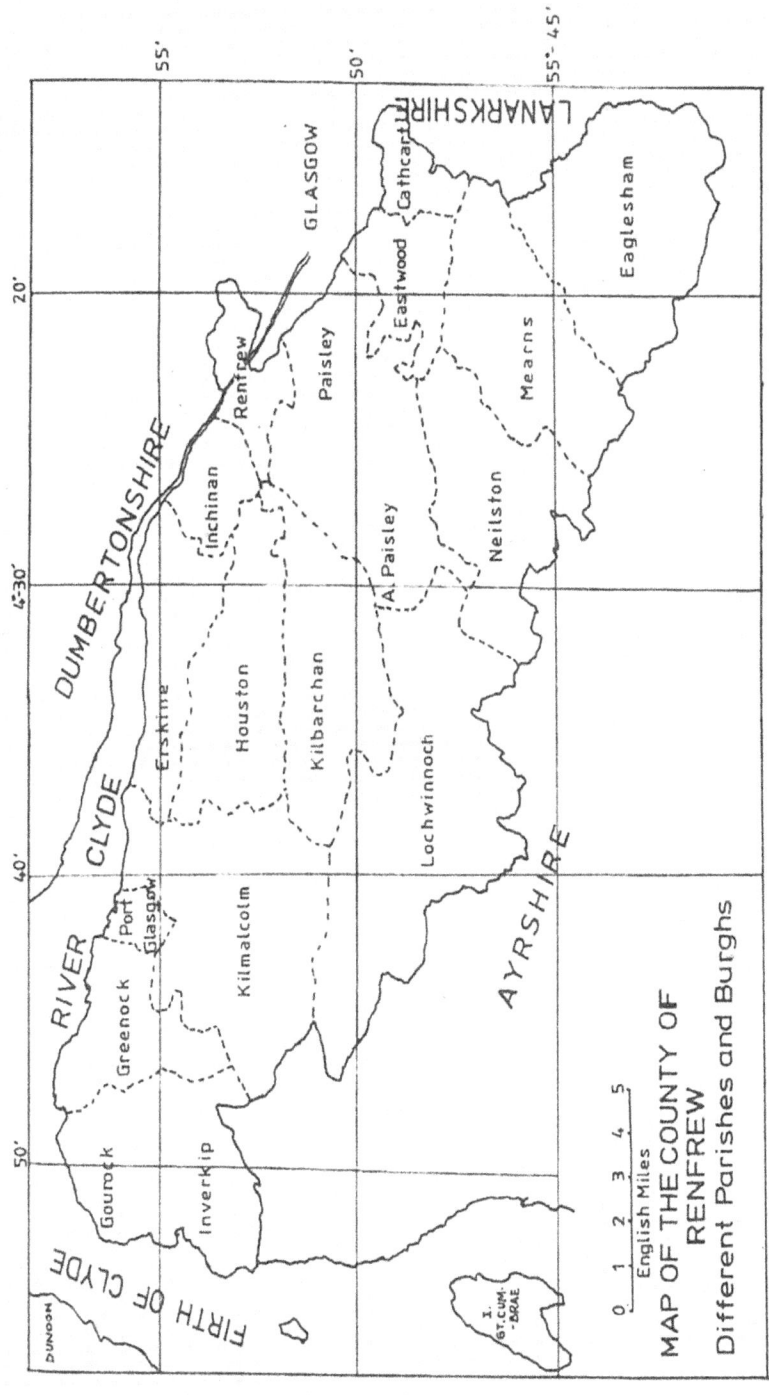

Chapter 1: Geographical, Social and Economic Background

1.1 Introduction

Geographical Features

The well-marked, natural divisions of Scotland were the Highlands, the Southern Uplands, and the Central Lowlands. They differed greatly from one another. The Central Lowlands were by far the country's most fertile and the main center of mining and manufacturing industries. It occupied a unique position in Great Britain, possessing the characteristics of three separate parts of England: the agricultural southeastern plain, the "Black Country" of West Midlands with its iron and coal, and Lancashire with its cotton manufactures. Dumbarton, Lanark, Ayr, and Renfrewshire were in this Central Lowland area. As Renfrewshire was on the western slope of Scotland, its position was not particularly advantageous for trade with Europe. However, by the mid-18th century, with the development of American trade, commerce shifted to the Atlantic shores, making Renfrewshire more important.[1]

Lanarkshire bordered Renfrewshire on the east and northeast and Ayrshire on the South. The river Clyde separated Renfrewshire from Dumbarton on the north, and the Firth of Clyde formed the western boundary.[2] The county was divided into seventeen parishes. Inverkip and Gourock were located in the western part of the county. Port Glasgow and Greenock were the vital port towns in the northern part of the county. Erskine and Inchinnan lay on the north part, bordered by the river Clyde. Kilmacolm, Houston, Killellan, and Kilbarchan formed the central part of the county, and Neilston, Mearns, and Lochwinnoch were situated in the southern part. Renfrew, Paisley, Eastwood, and Cathcart were all in the northwestern part, bordering Lanarkshire and Glasgow.

The county experienced remarkable growth as an industrial center during the second half of the 18th and first half of the 19th centuries. It became a central hub of textile manufacturing, thanks to its proximity to the iron industry and Lanarkshire and Ayrshire coalfields, allowing it to benefit from their development. The banks of the river Clyde, with good anchorage, were ideal for shipping and the ship-building industry. The county's mineral wealth in coal, iron, and lime, though not of the highest quality, provided a foundation for essential manufacturing industries of many kinds. Renfrewshire had plenty of good pastoral and agricultural land as well.[3]

1.2 Population Growth

Social and Economic Background

Renfrewshire was ranked as the twenty-seventh largest county among the thirty-three Scottish counties at the end of the 19th century. However, in terms of population, it was only exceeded by Lanarkshire and the cities of Edinburgh and Glasgow.

Renfrewshire had not always been so densely populated. In 1755, it was ranked seventeenth, and in 1791, it became tenth. By the mid-19th century, it had risen to sixth place among the counties considering population. In the second half of the 18th century, the county had only one-tenth of its inhabitants in the later part of the 19th century.[4] Table I shows the population growth in Renfrewshire and the different parishes from 1801 to 1871.

Table I:
Population of Renfrewshire from 1801–1871

Parish	1801	1811	1821	1831	1841	1851	1861	1871
Cathcart (pt)	1,050	1,449	1,885	2,082	2,141	2,734	3,635	7,134
Beith (pt)	-	-	67	65	45	41	37	-
Dunlop (pt)	-	-	68	56	76	74	55	-
Eaglesham	1,179	1,424	1,977	2,372	2,428	2,524	2,328	1,714
Eastwood	3,375	4,845	5,676	6,854	7,965	9,243	11,314	12,966
Erskine	487	963	973	973	1,144	1,394	1,457	1,565
Govan (pt)	-	-	550	710	1,528	3,096	8,870	?
Gourock	-	-	-	-	-	-	2,307	3,291
Greenock	17,458	19,042	22,088	27,571	36,936	37,436	43,894	58,817
Houston & Killellan	1,891	2,044	2,317	2,745	2,817	2,753	2,490	2,167
Inchinnan	462	641	582	642	678	649	619	584
Inverkip	1,367	1,632	2,344	2,088	3,399	3,018	1,188	937
Kilbarchan	3,751	3,563	4,213	4,806	5,595	5,474	6,348	6,093
Kilmacolm	1,130	1,474	1,600	1,613	1,616	1,399	1,455	1,716
Lochwinnoch	2,955	3,514	4,130	4,515	4,706	4,153	3,821	3,816
Levern	-	-	-	-	-	-	-	2,413
Mearns	1,714	1,914	2,295	2,814	3,088	3,704	3,547	3,543
Neilston	3,796	4,946	6,549	8,046	10,577	12,233	11,013	11,136
Paisley (burgh)	17,026	19,937	26,428	31,460	32,436	31,903	31,538	48,257
Paisley (Abbey)	14,196	16,785	20,575	26,006	28,051	28,549	29,687	11,988
Port Glasgow	3,865	5,116	5,262	5,192	7,377	7,027	7,294	10,823
Renfrew	2,031	2,305	2,648	2,833	3,076	3,898	4,684	5,908
Skelmorlie	-	-	-	-	-	-	-	886
	78,090	91,624	122,177	133,433	155,679	161,304	177,581	195,754

Sources: (1) N.S.A. 554
(2) Census of Great Britain-1831-Vol. II
(3) Census of Great Britain-1841-Vol. II
(4) Census of Great Britain- 1851-Vol. II
(5) Census of Scotland- 1861-Vol. II
(6) Census of Scotland-1871-Vol. II
(7) Census of Education for Scotland, Second Report 1875, 88.

The main reason for the rapid increase in population was the industrial revolution experienced by the county, which attracted many immigrants from other lowland counties of Scotland, the Highlands, Ireland, and even England. As a result of natural increase and migration, population growth was fast during the early decades of the 19th century. Till the 1830s, hand-loom weaving was at its peak in Paisley and Kilbarchan, and different manufacturers, ships, and shipbuilding prospered in the county. From 1841 until the 1860s, the area (Paisley in particular) was hit by economic depression. Moreover, Greenock lost most of her shipping to Glasgow due to the deepening of the River Clyde. As a result, the population increased only fractionally during this period. However, migration continued to a lesser extent, and there were out movements, especially from Paisley. By 1871, when shipbuilding flourished in Port Glasgow and Greenock, the industrial region experienced a further population influx.

In 1871, the area of Renfrewshire was 766,077,120 square miles, and the population density was 718.8 persons per square mile. Lanarkshire had 710.4 persons per square mile during that period. Ayrshire, in contrast, had only 173.1 persons per square mile.[5] Thus, it is clear that Renfrewshire had a very high population density by 1871. One of the crucial features of population growth was urbanization centered around the textile towns of Paisley, Neilston, and Eastwood and the port towns of Greenock and Port Glasgow. In the mid-19th century, there was virtually no population in the rural areas, indicating an outflow of population (Table 1). During the same period between 1831–71, the population doubled in Port Glasgow, Greenock, and Eastwood and grew in Paisley and Port Glasgow by 50%. As the population pressure became acute in these places, it was likely to affect the educational facilities provided for children.

During the 19th century, there was a significant influx of immigrants from various economic and social backgrounds into Renfrewshire. Despite some migration from Lowland Scotland, the Highlanders and the Irish movement were of greater importance for educational study. Industrial, social, political, and economic factors influenced the general population movement all over Britain. The migration from the Highland region began in the mid-18th century with the breakdown of the clan system. Many immigrants came to Paisley and Greenock, Glasgow, and Edinburgh.[6] This is confirmed by the significant Gaelic-speaking community in Paisley in the late 18th century, including a Gaelic Chapel. Similarly, a Highland Academy (a school for Highland children) was established in Greenock in the 1820s.

Paisley, along with Port Glasgow and Greenock, was favorably situated to tap the Highland and Irish population, offering employment in industries where wages were higher than in agriculture. Since no great skill was required (except in harness weaving) and there was no regular apprenticeship system, the influx of immigration was facilitated.

Most Highland immigrants to the Paisley and Greenock area came from Argyll and Bute. The Highlanders first settled in Greenock but eventually moved all over Scotland. Some found work in various trades and stayed in Greenock. Greenock had a larger Highland population than Glasgow and Dumbarton (Table II). R. D. Lobban,[7] M. McCarthy,[8] and M. Gray[9] have shown that geographical proximity was essential in the pattern of the Highland region.

Table II:
Proportion of Highlanders in Different Towns Between 1851–71

Year	Greenock	Glasgow	Dumbarton
1851	10.5%	4.7%	--
1871	8.6%	4.0%	3.9%

Source: Lobban, op. cit., 25.

In 1821, Paisley had 558 families of Highland origin, which accounted for just under 10% of the total number of families (5,730). The following most significant number (428) was from Argyll and Bute.[10] Table III shows the number of Highlanders who migrated into a "particular area" of Paisley from various parts of the Highlands in 1851.

Table III:
No. of Highlanders in a particular area in Paisley in 1851

Name of the County	Male	Female	Total
Argyll	56	71	127
Dumbarton (4 parishes)	1	2	3
Inverness	9	13	22
Ross and Cromarty	2	1	3
Sutherland	0	0	0
Stirling	1	0	1
Perth Forfar, Aberdeen	5	5	10
Banff, Moray, and Nairn (only Highland parts of the districts)	1	0	1

Source: Table II.A, Denis Docherty "The Migration of Highlanders into the Lowland Scotland 1780–1850, with Particular Reference to Paisley," (Unpublished B.A. dissertation, University of Strathclyde, (1976–7), 38.

There was a more significant influx of female immigrants than male immigrants (see Table IV). This was probably due to the demand for female labor in manufacturing industries. There was a definite concentration of Highland male and female migrants in the age group of 25 to 34, following the general migration pattern in Greenock.[11] The number of males and females of Highland origin and their percentage out of the total population in Greenock from 1801 to 1871 can be seen in the following table.

Table IV:
The number of men and women of Highland origin in Greenock between 1801–1871

Year	Men	Women	Total percentage of the Highlanders among the population of Greenock	
1801	2,483	2,617	5,100	29.0%
1841	1,912	2,148	4,060	11.0%
1851	1,942	2,182	4,124	11.0%
1871	2,491	2,687	5,178	9.1%

Source: Lobban, op. cit.; p. 455.

The Highlanders played an essential part in the economic revolution in Greenock and the Clyde estuary. Besides ordinary laborers, many skilled and semi-skilled workers came from the Highlands and settled there. They worked as porters, cart men, carpenters, coopers, shoemakers, tailors, weavers, and in many other trades and occupations. In particular, "the expansion of the mercantile marine and shipping of the Clyde region could not have taken place to the extent without the large reservoir of seamen in the Highlanders to operate the fleets"[12] till the mid-19th century. During the seasonal work, a group of shearers from the Highland region came down south for work. It is possible that some of them took up handloom weaving in Paisley for higher wages, but their numbers were relatively small. Most Highlander laborers worked on turnpike roads, railways, and canals. Some Highland women worked in domestic services or as plain weavers in the bleach fields and dye works. According to a Presbytery Report in 1837, there were 1,490 Highlanders in the countryside of Paisley, out of which 890 worked in bleach fields or print works, and the majority of them were women.[13]

In 1851, 10% of the population of Kilmacolm parish were Highland-born.[14] It is believed that the Highlanders migrated to an area to replace the locals who had moved to Greenock. According to the records of 1851 and 1881, in Renfrewshire, around 9,000 people were born in the crofting counties. Interestingly, the number remained the same even after 30 years. During the same period, almost 48% of all migrants from Argyll, Inverness, Ross, Cromarty, and Sutherland who moved into the Lowlands lived in either Renfrewshire or Lanarkshire.[15]

Irish immigration to Scotland, England, and America started in the 1790s. The main reasons for this immigration were the high population density, overworked and poor agricultural land, and increasing pressure on living standards in Ireland. Richard's and Dillon's studies on Irish immigration to Bradford and Leeds, respectively, confirm these causes.[16] Some scholars have also shown that earlier immigrant groups caused further movement out of Ireland to those areas. These were possibly the factors that also brought Irish settlers into Renfrewshire. It is difficult to ascertain which part of Ireland they moved from because they lack complete data or information. However, the 1851 census data for Paisley confirms that the areas from which the first immigrants came continued to supply more immigrants than other Irish counties (Table V).

Table V:
Birthplace of the Irish-born migrants in Paisley at selected points in terms of percentage from 1808–55

	1808-12(1)	1851 (2)	1855 (3)
Donegal Tyrone Londonderry	73	69	37
Antrim	4	12	13
Fermanagh Sligo Mayo	4	5	16
Other unspecified	20	14	25
N	69	83	231

(1) S. R. O. R.H. 21/8/9

(2) Paisley Census sample information, percentage as of those giving counties specified birthplaces only.

(3) S. R. O. 559/1-3573/1-3.

Source: Brenda E. A. Collins, Aspects of Irish Immigration into Two Scottish Towns (Dundee and Paisley) during the mid-nineteenth century (unpublished M. Phil thesis, Edinburgh University) 1979, 93.

In 1798, following the unsettled conditions in Ireland, the Irish landed in the western counties of Wigtown and Ayr and then spread through Renfrewshire and Lanarkshire in a northeastern direction. By 1841, Renfrewshire had the second-highest percentage of migrants at 13.2%, only being surpassed by Wigtownshire. The number of 20,500 was only second to that of Lanarkshire, with 56,000 Irish, which was 13.1% of the total population of that county.[17]

Another great wave of Irish migrants came after the Great Famine of 1847–48, when nearly 42,800 destitute Irish landed in Glasgow. They then spread to areas of Lanarkshire, as there was a growing demand for laborers in heavy industries, shipbuilding, and engineering. In 1861, in Renfrewshire, people of Irish origin numbered 24,955 out of a total population of 176,581, 14.1%. Lanarkshire had the highest proportion of Irish, with 14.6%, 93,394 out of a total population of 631,566. In 1871, the total increased slightly to 14.4%, 28,177 in Renfrewshire. The distribution of the Irish migrants had never been uniformed in the county. They concentrated mainly in Paisley and its neighboring towns of Barrhead, Johnstone, Neilston, Renfrew, Eaglesham, Lochwinnoch, Greenock, and Port Glasgow. The weaving town of Kilbarchan was exceptional in having few Irish among its 4,000 inhabitants, "the only instance," according to the N.S.A., "of a manufacturing village in the western district of a population exceeding 2,000 souls, with only 6 Catholics in that number."[18]

The Irish began to come to Paisley in considerable numbers from the beginning of the 19th century. The excavation of the Glasgow-Paisley-Johnstone canal in the first decade of the century brought many Irish who settled permanently in the town. However, it was as the chief center for the manufacture of fashionable and fancy cotton goods that Paisley attracted migrants. There was a substantial rise in the number of Catholics who were mainly Irish. There were only 861 Catholics when St. Mirren's Chapel was opened in 1808, which increased to more than 1,000 by 1816. In 1821, a census of the population of Paisley revealed that out of 5,730 families, 603 were Irish, 10.5% of all families. However, the number never increased more than 2% after 1841 in the town. The increase between 1841 and 1861 was 1%, while the increase in Renfrewshire was 13%. Paisley received fewer immigrant Irish laborers, as they were absorbed in shipbuilding and engineering industries in Greenock and Port Glasgow and, to a lesser extent, in Renfrew. A few small shipyards and engineering works provided employment to some in the town, and many of the female population worked in the thread works.[19] The number of Irish migrants in Paisley from 1821–71 can be seen in the following table (Table VI).

Table VI:

No. of Irish-born residents of Paisley, 1821–1871

Date	No.	Percentage of the total population
1821	5,170	11.00
1841	5,124	10.58
1851	5,439	11.34
1861	5,424	17.00
1871	4,645	10.00

Source: M. McCarthy, op. cit., Appendix N(a), 167.

In Greenock and Port Glasgow, the Irish had been settling since 1800. The number of Irish migrants in Greenock in the early 1830s was 4,000, with a population of 27,571. In August 1833, a heavy influx of Irish labor was reported between "two to three thousand weekly imported to the Clyde. In one week, not less than seven to eight thousand landed at Broomielaw."[20] Before that, several shipping merchants from Northern Ireland had either settled in the district or established agencies. At certain seasons, bands of laborers came to Greenock and returned home at the end of the harvest or other works. In 1841, the number was 4,307. According to J.E. Handley, the number was far more significant: "The number of Irish Catholics and Protestants in Greenock, including the total of seven years migrants over the years 1834–41, would be near to 6/7 thousand."[21] In 1871, the number of Catholics was 9,463 in a population of 58,817, 16.1%. The number of Catholics in Port Glasgow and Neilston is given in Table VII. The cotton spinning of Houston and Killellan also brought many Irish workers to that place. In Inchinnan, where they generally reaped the harvest, the Irish were seasonal migrants who arrived in great numbers during harvest time.

Table VII:

No. of Catholics in Port Glasgow and Neilston between 1835–6 to 1861

	1835–6			1861		
	Irish	Total population	%	Irish	Total population	%
Port Glasgow	332	5,192	6.4	2,431	7,294	3.3
Neilston	1,061	8,046	13.2	3,000	11,013	27.2

Source: William Forest Macarthur, *History of Port Glasgow*, (Glasgow, 1932), 223. David Pride, *History of the parish of Neilston*, (Paisley, 1910), 89.

Besides the Irish and Highlanders, many came from Glasgow, Lanark, Ayr, Dumbarton, and some even from England. There was an excellent opportunity for employment in textile weaving, non-weaving manufacturing, and other industries in Paisley and other areas of Renfrewshire. Many weavers from other textile areas in Scotland came to Paisley when the shawl trade prospered in the 19th century. Parkhill well expresses the contribution of weavers from Dunfermline and Edinburgh. A large number of migrants came from Ayr, Lanark, Stirling, and the Lothians. There were some 600 people from Ayrshire in a particular area in 1821. This continued to the second half of the century, when most migrants came from Ayr, Dumbarton, and Lanark counties. As the thread industry expanded, other works connected with textile industries also needed a large workforce. Parkhill, in 1856, wrote that the "population necessary to carry on increased manufactures was supplied from the Kilmarnock district and other parts of Ayrshire. Thus, in a great measure, Paisley was peopled from Ayrshire…"[22] A number of the prominent men who settled in Paisley and developed different industries were migrants to the town. Humphrey Fulton, founder of the town's silk industry, the Clark brothers, and James Coats, who developed machine thread, were all from Ayrshire. Their contribution towards the development of the town was invaluable. In 1851, in the whole of Renfrewshire, there were some 29,000 persons who had been born outside Scotland, and 38,000 had been born in other Scottish counties.[23]

Table VIII:

Proportion of Renfrewshire Inhabitants born Outside the County Expressed as a % of all Incomers

	Area of Birth	1841	1851	1881
1.	Adjacent counties (Ayr, Lanark, Glasgow, Dumbarton)	-	29	38
2.	Crofting counties (Argyll, Calton, Inverness, Orkney, Zetland, etc.)	61	13	9
3.	Other northern counties (Ross and Cromarty, Sutherland)	-	4	4
4.	Other Scottish counties (excluding Renfrewshire)	-	11	11
5.	England and Wales	3	4	5
6.	Ireland	34	38	31

Source: T.S.A., op. cit., III.

1.3 Industrial and Occupational Structure in Renfrewshire

The industries in Renfrewshire, like the whole of the Clyde basin, consisted of various manufacturing industries, including textile-weaving and non-weaving. Spinning and weaving had been carried on in the county for centuries for local consumption. "The whir of the spinning wheel and the clack of the loom had been heard in every county village" in the early 18th century. In the view of H.J. Habakkuk, the universal adoption of the power loom in the west of Scotland was quick because of the availability of an abundant and cheap labor supply.[24] This was due to an increase in population, the facility with which the trade could be entered, and the restriction on mobility. (In 1872, there were still 10,000 handloom weavers in that area.) A quarter of the Glasgow population was Irish and concentrated in the weaving areas of Carlton, BridgetOn, and Mile End. In Paisley, on the other hand, the harness loom was predominantly in operation, and that required high skill, with the result that unskilled migrant laborers could not enter into it very easily. The cost of the loom for hire was three pence per week, and paying a draw boy four shillings weekly was also an impediment to the impoverished Irish. Because of fancy weaving, few Irish draw boys were employed by harness weavers.[25]

Fancy weaving was relatively highly paid but was subjected to the whims of demand of fashion, which could be disastrous in times of slump. There were seasonal irregularities with peak times in autumn and spring, typical in the clothing trade. There was a lack of alternative employment, and the older weavers were very conservative and unwilling to take other jobs. However, in the country, agriculture or fishing could often supplement textile work in poor times. In Paisley, the great bulk of the regular weavers subsisted entirely by the loom. In the 1830s, according to N. Murray, one-third of Paisley's population depended on weaving. James Orr estimated that nearly half of the population depended on weaving then. Smout thought that almost half the population consisted of the families of the handloom weavers. At the same time, many of the rest were connected with weaving as designers of the patterned cloth or flower-lashers who prepared the harness looms before weaving. Others were engaged in starch making or producing weaver's reeds. So, more than half the population was connected directly or indirectly with weaving.[26]

In Kilbarchan, the handloom weaving industry peaked by 1830, when about 800 looms were used, as opposed to only 383 looms in 1791. Weaving was also the earliest industry in Barrhead of Neilston parish. There were some weavers in Eastwood, Houston Killellan, Lochwinnoch, Renfrew, Cathcart, and Eaglesham.

From the 1830s, the weaving industry suffered a gradual decline due to a falling demand for fancy goods, changes in fashion, economic depression, and competition from abroad. By June 1832, about 1,000 Paisley weavers were unemployed; in July, half of the Kilbarchan weavers had no web. Weavers' position suffered due to underemployment, and they continued to complain till 1833. However, with the railway boom of 1832–33 and the development of other industries, textile industries gained from the greater prosperity, and production increased. The downswing of the cycle began again in 1837. The Handloom Weaver's Commission reported in 1838 on the growing poverty and the declining prospects among the weavers of Paisley. In 1843, Sheriff Campbell recalled that half a dozen depressions had occurred in Paisley in the previous forty years.[27]

Thus, by 1842, unemployment and seasonal and cyclical variation of jobs almost transformed the weavers "into a State of literal starvation." In January 1843, 11,885 weavers were unemployed in Paisley. The industry experienced a short-lived revival in July 1848 at Paisley and Kilmarnock, but by the 1870s, it had almost disappeared. In 1871, 985 looms were still working, as opposed to 6,000 in 1830 (Table IX). There were still 200 looms at Kilbarchan in 1900, though the industry began to decline in the 1880s. In Eaglesham and other places, the weaving industry has declined since the 1860s.[28]

Table IX:

No. of Weavers in Paisley from 1830–80

Date	Weavers	Looms	Weavers	Looms	Notes
1830	-	6,000	-	1,717	This number includes the surrounding villages, with 2,000 in the villages.
1841	7000	-	-	-	
1854	2,922	-	1,217	-	
1861	800	2,536	746	-	
1871	-	985	-	566	
1880	946	-	107	-	

Source: M. McCarthy, op. cit., Appendix H, 162.

The famous staple of Paisley was the shawl, though the weavers also made clothing and dress materials. The shawl industry might be said to have represented a brilliant achievement by manual craftsmanship in the age of the machine. For instance, in their looms, Paisley weavers produced the effects of an Indian shawl by needle. Their work reached a marvelous height of prosperity, declined, and became extinct within eighty years (the 1810s).

The thread industry was another critical feature of Renfrewshire's industries in the 19th century, particularly of Paisley. Linen thread was produced initially, but it was replaced by cotton thread in the first decade of the century. In 1837, there were eight or nine steam-powered mills making cotton thread in Paisley. By 1873, the number had risen to 41. Mathew Blair commented about the principal developing industry of Paisley in the second half of the century, "It is to be feared that the industries which have created new Paisley have not preserved that artistic taste and culture which marked the epoch of handicraft work."[29]

However, the manufacture of cotton thread restored the town to solvency in 1873 after 30 years of bankruptcy. Coats and Clark dominated this manufacturing, and Paisley once again became a center of a world trade far more extensive than the silk or shawl industries. Other firms, except for Coats and Clark, rarely reached the eminence to dominate the markets.[30] In 1834, there were no cotton power looms in the town, but by 1838, there were 112.[31]

The cotton finishing trade increased in the 19th century in Renfrewshire. Materials were sent from Lancashire to get the benefit of the soft waters of the Cart and the skill of the Renfrewshire workmen. In 1834, there were 32 cotton factories in Renfrewshire outside Paisley. These were located mainly in Kilbarchan, Neilston, Houston and Killellan, Eastwood, Mearns, Kilmacolm, Lochwinnoch, and Cathcart. Even in Greenock and Port Glasgow, the central area of heavy industries, there were woolen and cotton manufacturers. Renfrewshire had taken a prominent place in manufacturing fine silk goods and cotton production. Many other works in connection with textile industries grew up in the county in the late 18th and early 19th century. In the 1850s, the primary industry of Eastwood parish was printing because of the availability of pure water. Bleaching, red dye finishing, and beetling were also carried out. The clear water of the Levern at Barrhead in Neilston Parish attracted print fields and bleaching works, which were further extended to calico printing and hosiery, taking advantage of the railway extension. There were print fields and bleaching works in places such as Kilbarchan, Mearns, Lochwinnoch, Eaglesham, and Cathcart. In Paisley, dying and bleaching were carried out mainly in the countryside.[32]

By the 1850s, all the larger towns in the county became important centers of the engineering industry. Paisley, Greenock, and Johnstone were the chief centers. Greenock was devoted to machine tools. All kinds of tools were made in the county. Different types of sugar refining machines were also produced. At Renfrew, there were the most significant water tube boiler works in Britain. One of the county's most extensive sanitary engineering works was in Barrhead. James Greenshields started Shale mining and oil distilling in the Linwood village of Kilbarchan in 1866. Many foundries in different parishes produced the largest castings needed for marine work. There were plants for breweries, distilleries, and white stone quarrying.[33]

The industries in Renfrewshire included sawmills, roperies, and works for sailcloth. Gourock Ropeworks of Port Glasgow, which was very famous, produced canvas and rope. There were a few corn flour mills in the county. At Paisley, starch, pottery, soap, and paper were made. Sugar works prospered in Greenock and Port Glasgow. In 1843, Greenock produced 50,000 tons of sugar. However, foreign competition and the introduction of the sugar beet to Britain in 1855 led to a local disaster. By 1873, British markets were flooded with beet sugar.

The Clyde Basin was the world's most significant shipbuilding center; Renfrewshire played a vital part in that industry. Greenock and Port Glasgow became very prominent as shipbuilding centers by the mid-19th century when foreign governments ordered shipbuilders to supply ships. The origin of Clyde's shipbuilding did not derive from skills but from the use of new techniques of propulsion and construction. Between 1812–20, 42 steam vessels were constructed on the Clyde. Other shipbuilding districts were also prospering from the simple assembly of engines and boilers. While the Clyde area produced 60% of the tonnage in 1812 in Britain, it dropped to 40% in 1821 (Table X).

Table X:

Steam tonnage built in Britain and on the Clyde, 1812–70 (all tonnage in '000 tons)

Period	Britain	River Clyde	% Clyde
1812–20	5.3	3.2	60
1821–30	30.5	4.2	14
1831–40	71.3	17.6	24
1841–50	122.6	81.4	66
1860–70	1,084.3	798.4	66

Sources: J. Strong, 'Social and Economic Statistics of Glasgow 1851-61', Glasgow Herald, 'Shipbuilding and Engineering Supplements' and G.R. Porter, Progress of the Nation, (London, 1851), 316, and A. Slaven, op. cit., 127.

By the 1830s, the simple assembly methods gave way to advanced techniques and efficient, skilled engineering, which pushed the lion's share back to the marine engineering of the Clyde. Coal and iron industries, which developed in Lanarkshire and Ayrshire, helped the rise of Clyde shipbuilding in the 1840s. There was a massive increase in Clyde, launching from 200,000 tons in 1860 to 342,000 in 1870, an increase from 33% to 55% of the British total.

By 1870, 24,000 out of 47,500 men employed in Britain's shipbuilding industry were in Scotland.[34] Industries connected with shipbuilding employed for 2/5 of the total working population in the 1860s in Port Glasgow and besides Port Glasgow and Greenock, Renfrew and Paisley also had a shipbuilding industry.

Greenock and Port Glasgow were significant ports of Scotland. The tobacco trade dominated Greenock and Port Glasgow along with Glasgow, in the 18th century. Until 1775, Port Glasgow was the leading port in Scotland with a flourishing tobacco trade with America and the West Indies. After this, foreign trade became more prominent in Greenock, with sugar, rum, molasses, and cotton replacing tobacco. The major export of this period was textile—linen until 1790, and cotton piece goods after that, with the West Indies, Low Countries, and France being the most valuable outlets. Greenock and Port Glasgow lost some of the trade to Glasgow after the improvement of navigation through the River Clyde in the 1840s. The deepening of the Clyde and the coming of the steamship resulted in more ships bypassing Greenock and sailing to Glasgow.[35] There was a change in the character of the trade, with basic food such as wheat, maize, and flour contributing half the inward tonnage. Trade in sugar and coal was confined to Greenock, and Port Glasgow dealt with the timber trade. In 1870, nearly 206,000 tons of raw sugar were landed in Scotland, nearly all in Greenock.

Besides industries and trade, a handful of people were engaged in agriculture and farming. The arable farms were mainly in Inchinnan and Erskine and differed from dairy farms. Dairy farms could be found in Houston, Killellan, Eaglesham, and in the landward areas of some other parishes in the county. Like Wigtown, Renfrewshire was one of the prominent dairy-farming shires in Scotland. The number of persons connected with agriculture and farming was negligible compared to people engaged in industrial pursuits. In 1831, 21,071 families out of 28,204 were in the manufacturing group, while only 2,016 were engaged in agriculture.[36] This pattern was also found in 1841 and 1871 (Table XI).

Table XI:

Number of persons in different occupations in 1871

Name of the occupation	Male	Female	Total
Industrial pursuit	58,545	32,469	91,014
Professional service (engaged in govt. service, army, navy etc.)	2,365	383	2,748
Domestic service (boarding, lodging and domestic service)	1,082	6,399	7,481
Commercial and conveyance	7,508	964	8,472
Agriculture, animal rearing and fishing	3,737	824	4,561
Manufacturing goods, mining and minerals	37,500	20,257	57,757
Indefinite class of laborers, independent pursuit and persons stating no occupations	6,353	3,642	9,995

Source: *Census of Scotland 1871, Vol. II-452.*

Male labor was prominent in shipbuilding and engineering while female labor was numerous in the textile sector. In Paisley, despite the depression, the textile industry was the main employer. The next largest group was shopkeepers and tradesmen, employing a third of the adult male labor. There was a small proportion of professional class workers, such as clergy, and doctors. Unskilled workers, mainly Irish, formed 15–20% of the male workforce. According to the Parliamentary Commission on the State of the Irish Poor in Great Britain (P.C.I.P.), the Irish were in great demand for their willingness, alacrity, and perseverance in the severe, most irksome and disagreeable kinds of coarse labor.[37] "I employed" stated a master spinner in 1834,

> in my spinning mill 279 hands, of whom 199 are Irish... I employed Irish from the beginning of the mill in 1810, they are the only people that asked for employment... They are hard working and industrious... if the Irish had not come here, we could not have got on without them.[38]

In the parliamentary investigation, another witness stated that, "It is my decided opinion that our manufacture never would have extended so rapidly if we had not had large importation of Irish families..." [39]

At the coarser and less skilled part of the manufacture of silk, cotton, woolen or ornamental fabrics in tanneries, foundries and construction works, the Irish migrants found employment. Some of them worked as stevedores at the docks in Greenock and Port Glasgow. A few were employed as ship carpenters, and some were engaged as farm laborers in agricultural areas. They formed almost the entire labor force in the sugar industry in Greenock and Port Glasgow. One sugar manufacturer stated, "If it were not for the Irish, we should be forced to give up trade and the same applied to every sugar house in the town, this is a well-known fact." Out of the 400 persons employed in the sugar houses of Greenock, 350 were Irish.[40] In addition, they were hawkers of fish, fruits, and hardware. The more prosperous of them took up business as secondhand dealers. Immigrant women worked in the cotton yarn mills, while the native women were employed on the cotton thread, higher in status. They also worked in different works connected with textile industries, and domestic services. The highlanders also played an important part in the economy of the Clyde region, though they were not so crucial and vital as in the late 18th century (Table XII).

Table XII:

Choice of occupation by Highlanders and Irish migrants in Greenock as shown in occupational categories in 1851

	Professionals	Domestic	Commercial	Conveyancing	Agriculture	Shop	Factories
Highlanders	5	0.6	1.7	17.4	4.2	14.9	56.2
Irish	1.1	0.2	0.3	17.9	3.6	16	60.9
Children of Highlanders	4.1	-	4.1	8.2	2.4	19.7	61.5
Children of Irish migrants	1.8	0.4	0.4	15.7	0.4	14.8	66.7
Norms	3.8	0.4	2.4	17.3	3	15.4	57.7

Occupation of the female Highlanders and Irish migrants

	Professionals	Domestic	Commercial	Conveyancing	Agriculture	Shop	Factories
Highlanders	1.1	64.1	-	-	1.9	29.5	3.4
Irish	0.5	28.6	-	-	0.8	31.3	38.8

Daughters of Highlanders	11.3	25.4	-	-	2.8	52.1	8.4
Daughters of Irish migrants	1.1	11.3	-	-	-	18.8	66.8
Norms	1.2	12.7	-	-	1.2	36.3	18.7

Source: 1851 Census Enumeration Book, Greenock 433–44.

There was a change in occupational structure among Irish children as well as in other groups. It is evident from the example of Paisley that more sons of Irish immigrants were in skilled jobs than their fathers. The percentage of sons in the unskilled sector among the Irish was far less than that of their fathers compared to non-migrant groups. Taking Paisley as a typical example of the county, some information about the wages of different groups has been given (Table XIV).

Table XIII:

Occupational distribution of co-residing sons and fathers in Paisley in 1851 by percent.

| | Migrant | | | | Non-Migrant | | All weighted | |
| | Irish | | Scottish | | | | | |
	Father	Son	Father	Son	Father	Son	Father	Son
Professional	2	-	15	-	10	3	11	1
Trade/Artisan	28	21	22	32	19	26	22	28
Textile (non-weaving)	10	29	10	22	3	16	8	12
Textile (handweaving)	21	24	34	17	45	26	37	21

	Migrant				Non-Migrant		All weighted	
	Irish		Scottish					
	Father	Son	Father	Son	Father	Son	Father	Son
Unskilled	38	22	15	7	19	19	20	14
Unemployed	-	-	-	7	-	-	-	5
Other	-	4	4	15	4	10	2	9
N (100%)	58		41		31		346	

Source: B. E. A. Collins, op. cit., Table 7. 9, 165.

Table XIV:

Adult male socioeconomic structure, (aged 20 and above), Paisley, 1851

	Income level (1)	Income stability (2)	Employment status (3)	Percentage (%)
Professional	H	R	SE	4
Artisan/Shopkeepers	M	RIC	SE/E/Ed	25
Textile (non-weaving)	MIL	SIC	Ed	17
Textile (handweaving)	LIM	RIC	SE/E/Ed	28
Other, factory employment	MIL	C	Ed	2
Unskilled	L	SIC	SE/Ed	15
Others	-	-	-	9

(1) H-High, M-Medium L-Low

(2) R-Regular, C-cyclical S-seasonal

(3) SE-self-employed, £-employers, Ed-employed.

Source: B.E.A. Collins, op. cit., Table 7.1, 132, same scheme is adopted in M. Anderson, *Family Structure in Nineteenth Century Lancashire*, (Cambridge, 1971), 26.

In handloom weaving, the lowest paid were the weavers of buckram, other coarse lining materials, and plain cotton handloom weaving. Higher wages were paid to the weavers of the "plain middles" of shawls, made of fine silk thread. Harness loom-made cotton shawls of cheaper materials, which required high skill and the assistance of a draw boy, were highly paid (Table XV). It should be mentioned here that, during peak times in the early 1830s, the heavy-figured shawl (harness) weavers used to earn £3 weekly. And even the Irish in the less skilled job of cotton spinning could get 25/- per week.[41]

Table XV:

Net weekly wages for different classes of woven goods in Paisley, 1830–50

4/-	6/-	10/-	13/-
Buckram lappets (plain goods)	-	Light-figured shawls (harness)	-
-	Cotton shawls (harness), plain middles (silk)	-	Heavy-figured shawls (Harness)

Sources: *PP 1835 xiii*, *Symons Report* 28–35. Dr. Harding's *Report* 186–9, B.E.A. Collins, *op.cit.*, Table 7.2, 139.

The wages of some non-weaving sectors were higher than the weaving sectors but offered little employment for adult males (Table XVI). One quarter of the print work adult labor force were block printers whose wages were from 20/- to 25/- per week in the 1840s. Railways and construction provided the primary employment for the skilled merchants. The wages in Glasgow of different groups are given below (Table XVII and XVIII), which probably are representative of other west of Scotland towns, like Paisley, Greenock, and Port Glasgow.

Table XVI:

Net weekly wage rates in the textile trade (non-handweaving) in Paisley 1830–1855

	Males		Females		Children
10/-	Print field laborers	5/-	Bleach field worker	2/-	Piercer, calendar worker
15/-	-	-	Stove girl, redder	-	-
10/-	Calendar worker	7/6	Shawl, warehouse, sewer	5/-	Drawboy, thread factory worker, tearer
25/-	Cotton spinner, silk millworker, block printers (gross)	-	-	-	-
30/-	Engraver, pattern drawer, block cutter.	-	-	-	-

Sources: PP 1843 xv, PP 1887, lxxxix, Return relating to wages, 273, B.E.A. Colfins, op. cit., Table 7.3.

Table XVII:

Selected daily wage rates of Glasgow in 1850, non-textile employment only

2/6	3/6	4/-	5/-
Laborers	Mason, Slater, Pattern maker	Millwright, House carpenter	Bricklayer

Sources: PP 1887 lxxxix 273, B.B.A. Collins, op. cit., Table 7.4, 146.

Table XII:

Average wages per week—Glasgow area, 1831–70

	1831	1851	1870
Blacksmiths	17/-	22/-	26/-
Carpenters	14/-	20/-	27/-
Colliers	13/-	15/-	28/-
Laborers	9/-	12/-	14/-
Machine workers	19/-	22/6	-
Masons	14/-	18/-	26/-
Female spinners	15/-	-	19/-
Male spinners	24/-	25/-	26/-
Weavers (hand)	6/6	6/-	-
Agricultural worker (annual)	£12	£29	£41
Married plowman (West of Scotland)	-	£17.10	£36

Sources: J. Cleland, *Enumeration of the inhabitants of Glasgow*, etc., J. Strong, 'The Wages of Labour,' op. cit., 1851 and 1856. A.L. Bowley, 'Statistics of wages in the United Kingdom during the last hundred years, agricultural wages,' Journal of the Royal Statistical Society, 62, 1899, A. Slaven, op. cit., Table 17, 156.

The carpenters in Greenock and Port Glasgow shipyards were getting from £1- to £1.1/- weekly in the 1840s and 1850s. The sawyers received £1.5/- per week with 10 hours of work per day. In sugar refineries, the wages were high for skilled workers (up to £1.10/-), while the ordinary laborers received wages starting from 12/- upwards. The wages of a plowman with bed, board, and washing in Erskine per half year was £12.10/- in the 1840s. The farm servants used to get £7.11/- half yearly. According to P.C.I.P. witnesses, the highest wages for female labor were in sewing or fringing shawls for warehouses, but they were liable to demand fluctuations. The next highest was in thread work. The wages were lowest in cotton spinning mills, bleach, and print works, 5/- to 7/- per week. Female servants in agricultural areas were getting £3.14/- to £5 per half year.[42]

1.4 Conclusion

In the 19th century, the population of Renfrewshire increased at a rapid rate. However, the growth rate was sluggish at times. Emigration from Ireland and the Scottish Highlands and population movement from neighboring counties added to natural growth, resulting in a faster growth rate. The county faced economic depression in the 1840s and 1850s, and the out-movement of the population to different areas of Britain and Canada slowed the growth rate. Despite this, Renfrewshire became a densely populated county during the 19th century. On the contrary, there was little growth in the rural areas, and urbanization concentrated the population mainly in five towns. The county was an area subjected to economic fluctuations strongly related to textile industries, with periods of severe depression for the leading occupational group in the first half of the century. Nonetheless, it was also an area where there were other opportunities with the growth of heavy industries. There was a wide variation in wages among the different occupational groups. This population growth and economic condition were likely to affect the children's education in the county, especially in the urban areas, between 1830 and 1872.

Chapter 2: The Denominational Role in Education in Renfrewshire

2.1 The Role of the Established Church in Education in Renfrewshire

2.1.1 Introduction

The framework of pre-industrial society was essentially religious in Scotland and, to a significant extent, was under church control. However, the Industrial Revolution had such an impact on society that the very character of the society was to be drastically changed. With industrialization, the 19th century saw the gradual disintegration of the control of the Established Church over society and education. Besides, the American and French Revolution greatly affected Britain's political and social sphere. Many educated classes began to see the importance of education in economic terms. In this connection, the names of Adam Smith, Lancaster, Bell, Owen, Birkbeck, and others were significant.

In the 19th century, humanitarianism, enlightened self-interest, and the necessity for social control guided Scotland's middle-class idea of education. The business community believed education would make a man a good worker and raise industrial output.[1] In Europe, many countries had begun a national scientific and trade education system. In Scotland, by the mid-19th century, the middle classes became aware that the parish school system, devised when Scotland was a rural and village society, was unworkable in industrial society. By 1860, even religious men became aware that the Established Church was not powerful enough to retain control of education.

The Power and Control of the Presbytery

The Education Act of 1803 maintained the connection between the Established Church and the parish schools. The minister continued to play his role in the selection, fixing of salary, and deciding the duties of the master. The presbytery, with some restrictions, was to examine and approve the candidate's religious orthodoxy and could deal with those masters reported by ministers and heritors as "guilty of misdemeanor."[2] In Renfrewshire, the appointment of the masters of parochial and some non-parochial schools had to be approved by the presbyteries of Greenock and Paisley till 1861. In the case of Eaglesham and Cathcart, it was to be done by the Presbytery of Glasgow. The decision of the presbytery was final and without appeal to any court, civil or ecclesiastical.

After establishing the Reformed Church of Scotland in the mid-18th century, all the parishes in Renfrewshire except Eaglesham and Cathcart were formed into the Presbytery of Paisley. That was the only presbytery in the county till 1834, when, by a deed of the General Assembly, a second presbytery was instituted in the lower ward of the county known as the presbytery of Greenock, containing Inverkip, Greenock, Port Glasgow, and Kilmacolm. Cathcart and Eaglesham continued to remain under the Glasgow Presbytery.

All the presbyteries were required to send a list of schools within their boundary to the General Assembly since 1799. They were to report on the taught subjects and how the schools were maintained. The responsibilities of the organization of inspection and reporting were taken over by the Educational Committee (E.C.C.) organized in 1824 by the Assembly. In 1836, the assembly instructed the committee "to revise and enlarge the schedule on which the presbytery reports the yearly examination of scholars within their bounds." The report was a printed schedule containing several inquiries regarding education sent by the presbytery to the parish minister, which he was to answer. It was then published by the presbytery and sent to the E.C.C. Sometimes. However, the reports were taken, they were not published. In 1837, the presbyteries of Paisley and Greenock had made reports on 11 parochial and 44 other schools, of which the reports of five parish and 12 other types of schools were published.[3] It may be pointed out that probably all schools did not comply in submitting reports or answering the queries of the minister.

The schools were also inspected and periodically examined by the presbyteries. In 1837, 80 schools [out of 111 schools] were inspected by the Committee of the Presbyteries in Renfrewshire, and 92 schools were periodically examined. In the case of the Burgh schools, which were under the town councils, the minister and the magistrates, council members, and eminent men were a part of the examination. Often the masters of subscription or adventure schools did not like these examinations. According to J. Hutton, schoolmaster of Thornliebank Village School, Eastwood, his school was examined by the clergy of the Church of Scotland, who assumed the right but whose authority he did not recognize.

By 1839, the procedure of the church examination was fairly routine. The presbytery usually appointed a committee of two to three clergymen, including the parish minister and some heritors. Parents of the children often attended the examination. The visitors watched while the master conducted the lessons, most of which might have been previously prepared. Most historians argue that this would have had a good effect as the master would have been reminded that others cared for his work and would encourage him to give full efforts in his teaching.[4]

In 1839, a Committee of the Privy Council (C.C.E.) was formed to control the government grant award initiated in 1833. The Committee decided to appoint inspectors who would recommend the award of the building grant. The opposition to this measure argued that it attempted to make the schools and masters "completely amenable and subservient to the caprices, crotchets, and arbitrary orders of the committee."[5] The Church of Scotland was also against granting money to schools directly based on government inspection, as it would undermine the privileges of the church, and they believed it was against the spiritual interest of the people. The government finally compromised, and concessions were made to the Anglican Church in England that all appointment of school inspectors had to be approved by the archbishop. The denominational control in inspection in Scotland was mainly a product of English affairs. In Scotland, the E.C.C. proposed that the church be consulted before the appointment of inspectors was accepted by the C.C.E. The influence of the church in education became weaker when the Disruption occurred. In 1843, a third of the ministers at the General Assembly seceded from the Church of Scotland (over patronage and other issues) and formed the Free Church of Scotland.[6]

By the mid-19th century, Scotland had movements for "educational reforms on a comprehensive legislative and national scale." The radical liberal middle class became aware that the parish school system was not ideal for an industrial society and sought greater state control. Another reason for the demand for state-controlled education was that the Church of Scotland was no longer the only national church after the Disruption. The increasing influence of the central government of Westminster in education made Scottish middle-class people aware of the need for educational reforms in Scotland.

The Church of Scotland opposed any reform of the Scottish educational system, which would diminish its complete control over the parish schools. By 1853, the church, the landed gentry, and the aristocracy were trying to organize vigorous opposition to any change in educational policy. Already in 1849, the General Assembly drew up "a Protest Declaration and Testimony of the subjects of National education."[7] It formed a committee to watch over bills and petitioned against any relaxation on religious tests for teachers and all other measures.

The church condemned the 1854 Education Bill, which proposed the establishment of a Board of Education for Scotland to control all parochial and public schools. It would appoint inspectors, prepare rules and regulations, and present reports to Parliament through the Committee of Education. Opponents saw in the bill the dissolution of the connection between the Church of Scotland and the parish schools, and ultimately, the bill was defeated. Finally, the Education Act of 1861 "wrung the minimal concession from the obdurate Church of Scotland" and opened up the offices of parochial schoolmasters to teachers of other denominations. It removed the power of the presbytery to make a parish schoolmaster accept the confession of faith. The examination of the masters was transferred to the Board of Examination, and they were to be tried by the sheriff. Only the approval of the presbyteries was necessary to make a report by the H.M. Inspectors on minor offenses of the teacher. They also could complain to the secretary of state about religious instruction and might continue to visit schools within their bounds. The General Assembly condemned the Education Act when it was passed, protested against it, and sent a petition to the House of Commons.[8]

The Contribution of the Established Church to Education in Renfrewshire

The assessment of the Established Church's contribution to children's education during the period under study is based primarily on the parliamentary returns of schools of 1841, 1854, 1862, and 1867. Basic information obtained therein, though, provides detailed information on the faith of the students and teachers, number of scholars, subjects taught, fees, and other related information.

Before the beginning of the 19th century, there was a parochial school in most of the parishes in Renfrewshire. Only the parish school at Gourock was erected in the second decade of the century. These schools were erected by the heritors and were controlled by them and the Church of Scotland. Besides, the church ran eight other schools in 1836–7. In 1865, the number was fourteen, including four side schools in the county outside Paisley and Greenock. There were 21 schools in Paisley and Greenock connected with the church. The schools controlled by the church were of different kinds. Inchinnan, Lochwinnoch, and Port Glasgow were female industrial schools. Others were infant and sessional schools. There was a school at Busby in Cathcart under the church's control in 1837. The returns of 1861 confirm that the church still controlled the school and was getting a grant for the certificated teachers.[9] But in the returns of 1867, there is only a reference to Busby Works School (undenominational) and Busby Catholic School, both in the parish of Mearns. There is no mention of the Busby Established Church school, which probably had been discontinued.

Although the E.E.C. had been formed in 1824 in Scotland, it was not until 1836 that a school in Renfrewshire could be established. However, it is evident from the data available that its activities were limited to Paisley and Greenock. The committee was initially set up to provide schools in the highland parishes and offered to set up "assembly schools." The aim was to complement the parish schools and to make them "essentially and effectively bible schools."[10] The heritors were obliged to build a school building and a master's house and provide other costs, while the E.C.C. would provide a salary for the teacher ranging from twenty pounds or more. Moreover, these schools were to be established at least three miles away from a parish school. From 1837, with the help of parliamentary grants, these schools were erected in the Lowlands. The committee founded two schools in Low and High Church parishes in Paisley in the late 1830s for cheap elementary education on Christian principles.[11] The committee paid £15 per annum (less than it had to pay) to its teachers, who also collected the fees. Two such schools were located in Greenock. There is no evidence whether the heritors provided these schools and masters' houses.

Another kind of school introduced by the church was the "Sessional School," in which the master was appointed and paid by the individual kirk session of a town parish. These were generally large schools operated on the monitorial system. The monitors carried out some teaching duties and had to arrange books and slates every morning.[12] In 1860–61, there were three sessional schools in Paisley, which received a privy council grant for certificated teachers. Two such schools in Greenock received a grant for a pupil-teacher.[13]

Quite a large part of elementary education depended on Sunday Schools in the 19th century, due to the demands for children as factory laborers. In 1807, according to David Stow, the whole population of Paisley could read and write. After a decade, as weaving shops required the help of the children, 3,000 children and many adults were illiterate.[14] As a result, children depended on Sunday schools for instruction. Sabbath schools multiplied in towns and county parishes. In 1837 in Renfrewshire in all parish and other Established Church schools, Sunday schools were held under the guidance of the church. At that time, an association was formed at Paisley town with members chiefly drawn from the Established Church. It employed three licentiates of the church to work in the populous areas of the town and the Abbey parishes. The Sabbath School Society was established in 1796 and was supported by members of different denominations. In 1833, one society completely supported by the members of the Established Church emerged. It increased the number attending Sabbath schools in Paisley. The attendance rose from 2,000 to 4,198 in 1840.

The Female Industrial Schools supported by the church had female teachers, and the girls were taught sewing, knitting, and music, with some reading and writing in some of them. The church mainly fostered the erection of female schools in Scotland. Dr. Andrew Bell,[15] who was an army captain, went to India and devised his Madras system there, leaving in his will a large amount of money for educational purposes. The E.C.C. received its share for schools running under the Madras system. In 1861, one such school was erected in Neilston by Rev. Hugh Aird, the parish minister. The school received grants of £100 each from the Bell trustees, the Ferguson Bequest, and the government grant. The rest of the required money was raised by public subscription.[16] The school was under the management of the minister and the kirk session.

The Report of the A.C.II on the number of scholars in different schools in Renfrewshire reveals that the church, with 13 parish schools, had 1,761 scholars in 1865. There were 1,469 children in another 14 schools under the church outside Paisley and Greenock in the 1860s.[17] It controlled the education of nearly a third of the total scholars inside that area (3,230 out of 10,019 scholars). In 1854, in Paisley, the church, with 19 schools and 1,911 scholars out of a total number of 5,157 scholars, was responsible for the education of nearly two-fifths (37.05%) of the scholars, while in Greenock, it had 6% of the scholars with only 198 out of 3,244 students.[18]

Precise determination of the role played by the Established Church on improvements of educational standards during the period under study is impossible because of the absence of detailed information on all the schools in the area. One can only draw tentative conclusions based on available data from 1841 and 1867 for parish schools, assuming changes therein reflect the changes in Renfrewshire. The report of the S.C.E.S. 1841 reveals only the number of scholars on the roll, while the Argyle Commission Scotland's second report (A.C.II) of 1867 adds the number of students in actual attendance to the number of students on the roll. Comparison of these two sets of data would increase the number of scholars, but it should also be borne in mind that the increase in the figures could also result from an increase in population data. Table XIX shows the number of scholars in different parish schools in 1837 and 1865.

Table XIX:

Data of scholars in parish schools in Renfrewshire for the years 1837 and 1865

Name of the parish	Students on Roll	
	In 1837	In 1865
Cathcart	33	130
Eaglesham	28	116
Erskine	80	93
Eastwood	105	251
Houston and Killellan	47	66
Gourock	38	69
Inverkip	64	141
Inchinnan	46	62
Kilbarchan	57	176
Kilmacolm	27	137
Lochwinnoch	90	176
Mearns	121	98
Neilston	161	237
Total	897	1,752

Sources: PP. 1841 xix 261–67 and PP. 1867 xxvi 212–17.

In the 28 years between 1837 and 1865, there was an increase of 855 scholars or a 95.32% increase. The population figures for different parishes are presented in Table XX. Between 1831–61, the total population in the 13 parishes rose by 16,161, from 39,550 to 51,522, an increase of 30.27%. Thus, comparing the 30.27% increase in population with the 95.32% increase in the number of scholars in parish schools, one can conclude that there was an increase in the number of children receiving education in these schools in Renfrewshire.

It is challenging to assess the quality of education imparted in the church schools. However, if the information on the subjects taught and the teacher's qualification (whether he or she was certificated or not) can be correlated, then some valuable conclusions can be derived.

Table XX:
Population in different parishes in Renfrewshire

Name of the Parish	Population	
	1831	1861
Cathcart (part of)	2,082	3,635
Eaglesham	2,372	2,328
Erskine	973	1,457
Eastwood	6,854	11,314
Houston and Killellan	2,745	2,490
Gourock	-	2,307
Inverkip	2,088	1,188
Inchinnan	642	619
Kilbarchan	4,806	6,348
Kilmacolm	1,613	1,455
Lochwinnoch	4,515	3,821
Mearns	2,814	3,547
Neilston	8,046	11,013
Total	39,550	51,552

Sources: Census of Great Britain Vol. II-1831, Census of Scotland Vol. ll-1861 Note: There was no mention of the population of Gourock separately in the 1831 Census. It was included in the Inverkip area, though it had a separate parish school from 1819. In 1885, Gourock was separated from Inverkip'

In 1837, English, reading, writing, arithmetic, grammar, mathematics, religion, Latin, history, and geography were provided in all the parish schools except for two schools where only reading, writing, and religion were taught. Some had instruction in bookkeeping, Greek and modern languages, navigation, and land surveying. In other types of church schools, except for two female Industrial Schools, the primary requisites in those days, reading, writing, and arithmetic (with religion), were imparted with some of them including history and geography.[19]

Finally, suppose one compares the efforts of the church in Renfrewshire with those in Ayrshire and Stirlingshire regarding the number of schools belonging to the church and the proportion of them receiving grants for certificated teachers. In that case, it is clear that Renfrewshire fares better marginally regarding trained teachers, while the church was more active in erecting schools in those two other areas (Table XXI, XXII). Although attendance ratios do not reflect the contribution of a particular organization, it is interesting to note that the church schools had a fractionally better record than those two counties' (Table XXIII).

Table XXI:
Percentage of Schools belonging to Established Church out of the total schools in Ayrshire, Renfrewshire, and Stirlingshire in 1865.

County	Church Schools	Total Schools	%
Ayrshire	45	249	38
Renfrewshire	48	195	25
Stirlingshire	43	165	27

Source: PP. 1867 xxvi, PP. 1854 lix.

Table XXII:
No. of schools (parochial and others) receiving grants for certificated teachers in Ayrshire, Renfrewshire, and Stirlingshire under the authority of the Church of Scotland in 1865.

Parish	No. of schools receiving such grant			Total schools			
	Parochial	Other schools	Total	Parochial	Other schools	Total	%
Ayrshire	17	9	23	43	54	97	24
Renfrewshire	9	7	16	13	35	48	33
Stirlingshire	8	6	14	23	22	45	31

Source: PP. 1863 xlvi, 100–103.

Table XXIII:
Percentage of scholars attending Church of Scotland schools in Ayrshire, Renfrewshire, and Stirlingshire in 1865 out of the total children on roll.

County	No. of children attending school	Total children on roll	%
Ayrshire	8,362	10,586	79
Renfrewshire	2,362	2,910 (1)	81
Stirlingshire	3,027	3,757	80

(1) Outside Paisley and Greenock, and a part of Paisley. Source: PP. 1867 xxvi, 37–50, 212–24.

2.2 The Contribution of the Heritors Toward Education

The famous Education Act of 1696 stipulated that heritors of each parish in the realm should meet, provide a commodious house for a school, and arrange a salary for the master, which should not be under 100 marks. The teacher's salary was to be met by a tax on the local heritors and tenants. The Education Act of 1803 outlined these duties: the salary was raised to ¾ hundred marks, and the heritors were made responsible for providing a dwelling house for the master. Two significant changes were outlined in this legislation. First, the share of the control with the Church of Scotland in all decisions concerning the parish schools was confined to those landowners whose landholding was more than £100 Scots in value. Secondly, section two of the act permitted the heritors to split a large and densely populated parish and establish an additional school in that part.[20] The Act of 1838, "to facilitate the Foundation and Endowment of additional schools in Scotland," provided that the heritors had to supply the school building and master's house of the additional school, and the government then would extend a salary to the teacher. The schools built under the 1803 and 1836 acts were known as side schools.

In 1852, Renfrewshire had 112 heritors in different parishes holding more than £100 Scots in value. The number of them in each parish was as follows:

- Dunlop (part of) — 1
- Abbey Paisley — 17
- Cathcart — 4

- Eaglesham — 2
- Greenock — 3
- Houston and Killellan — 5
- Inchinnan — 5
- Inverkip — 4
- Kilbarchan — 10
- Kilmacolm — 7
- Lochwinnoch — 9
- Mearns — 11
- Neilston — 12
- Port Glasgow — 1
- Renfrew — 9[21]

A couple of heritors in Eaglesham kept the school in running condition, while Abbey Paisley and Renfrew with a large number of heritors—seventeen and nine respectively—had no parish schools. Rev. R. Macnair wrote in the N.S.A. that in "Abbey Paisley, of the thirty-two schools, not one is parochial… the heritors of the Abbey had resolved to assess themselves in the legal sum of three chalders for the support of three parochial teachers each to be allocated in one of the three districts of the parish—in East, West, and middle."[22] It is unknown whether the plan materialized, as no further evidence exists. In Greenock, in the mid-18th century, the parish school was discontinued. There was no parish school in Port Glasgow, perhaps because of the smaller number of heritors in the parish, which was probably true of earlier centuries. The heritors erected four side schools in Renfrewshire in the mid-19th century. One such school was located in the Quarrelton village of Abbey Paisley; others were in Kilmacolm, Mearns, and Lochwinnoch. Kilmacolm had no other school besides the parish and the side school.

The Act of 1861 increased a teacher's salary to £30 per annum, for which the heritors were responsible. The total amount paid by the heritors in Renfrewshire in 1863 was £427-18s-2d, under Act 43 Geo 3, c 54. They also contributed additional money of £349-4s-4d, including the allowance to the female teacher under the Act 24 and 25 Vict, c 107.[23.] If the burghs of the county can be excluded, then of the remaining 13 parishes, the total salary of the masters would amount to £390, taking £30 per annum as the minimum salary. In 1837, the S.C.E.S. report shows that most parish schoolmasters enjoyed a salary of £30 or more. It was £20 and £25 in Gourock and Erskine, respectively. Thus, the heritors provided more than they were required by law.

By the 1840s, the heritors had provided a dwelling house for the master in most cases. The house provided often had two or three rooms, a kitchen, and sometimes a garden. The master of Inchinnan Parish School got a house consisting of four rooms and a kitchen. In Mearns, the master's house comprised five rooms and a garden. An excellent master's house was erected in 1830 by the heritors to replace the older one in Neilston. In some cases, the master was given money instead of a house. The heritors had a controlling voice in the fixing of the master's salary, determination of the school fee, and preparation of the curriculum. They also controlled the subjects upon which the master was examined. The masters were appointed by the heritors after being chosen by the minister and examined on subjects "required by the Heritors" by a committee selected by the presbytery.

The heritors also had the power to dismiss the parish schoolmaster. In Neilston and Kilbarchan, the master was dismissed because he did not know Latin, although he could teach English and arithmetic.[24] In some cases, they played only a part in appointing a master of other schools. In the Linwood Company's school in

Kilbarchan in 1837, the master was appointed by the company upon the advice of the principal inhabitants. The principal inhabitants would include the landlords. These duties and powers without provision of contributing money were transferred in 1872 to the School Boards.

2.3 Conclusion

The heritors, the presbytery, and the kirk session of the Established Church were all deeply involved in running schools. They were particularly conscious of their role in inspecting what was taught in the schools. Still, in many places, the church's efforts proved inadequate in maintaining the provision of schools to match the rapidly growing population. While the heritors were able to provide reasonable accommodation in smaller parishes, in the growing towns of Greenock, Port Glasgow, and Renfrew, they failed to fulfill their obligations. Moreover, in Greenock, Port Glasgow, and Renfrew, schools run by the church came nowhere near fulfilling the need.

In Scotland, there was the radical liberal middle class who sought state provision of education. The Established Church was against any educational reform undermining its authority over parish schools and education. However, the church was ultimately forced to give up its control over the parish schools in 1861, though the heritors continued to increase the salary of the parish teachers till 1872.

Chapter 3: Structure of Education: The Denominational Role in Education in Renfrewshire

3.1 The Role Played by the Free Church in Education in Renfrewshire

3.1.1 The Free Church in Scotland and Renfrewshire

In 1843, the Free Church was established nationally due to a secession from the Established Church due to factional controversies. While some may argue that the disruption happened due to the question of patronage, in reality, the moderates and two of the evangelicals had differences on more than just the patronage issue. It went much deeper than just that. "It was cleavage between two incompatible philosophies of life."[1] The ministerial support for the Free Church in Scotland came from socially and geographically diverse sources. It was strong in the Synod of Ross, Sutherland, and Caithness, north of the Highlands, where the secession was as high as 65–75%.[2]

In the southern Synods of Merse, Teviotdale, Galloway, and Dumfries, the percentage of the secessionists was as low as 25, 22, and 19%, respectively. The reason was that in the northern Highlands, most of the population lived by subsistence agriculture and had no security. These areas were affected by clearances and evictions, and the Church of Scotland had become closely associated with the interests of the landlords in many minds.[3] Thirty-nine to forty percent of the seceding clergy members of these areas were members of the endowed churches and supported wholeheartedly by the depressed peasantry.

The support for the Free Church originated from the prosperous city ministers. Although in the Synod of Glasgow and Ayr, 41% of ministers seceded, in the predominantly urban presbyteries of Greenock and Glasgow, the majority entered the new church—12 out of 16 and 31 out of 58, respectively. In the Synod of Lothian, Tweeddale, the seceders had a majority in the presbyteries of Edinburgh (34 out of 55) and Haddington (11 out of 20). The majority changed their allegiance to the Free Church in the Synod of Angus and Mearns. Fifteen out of twenty-eight came out of the Church of Scotland in the presbytery of Dundee, and in the city of Aberdeen, the number was 15 out of 15.

In Renfrewshire, many meeting places of the church were established in villages and townships. In the presbytery and Paisley, the number of seceders was probably like that of the Synod, 40–41%. In Paisley town, by 1850, six new Free Churches existed. As an educationist, Mr. William Fraser, the minister of the Free Middle Church, played an essential part in Paisley and was elected as a member of the Board at the first School Board election in 1872. In Mearns and Erskine, Free Churches were erected in 1843. In 1845, the minister of Gourock Parish Church at Durrocks also seceded. In Lochwinnoch, the then-member of the parish church, Dr. Smith, led the formation of the Free Church.[4] In some of the parishes of the presbytery, the Free Church failed to erect a church.

In the presbytery of Greenock, on the other hand, the constitutionalists, or the moderate party, were in the minority. When the Secession occurred, all the parish churches under the presbytery became vacant except in Port Glasgow, Inverkip, and East Greenock.[5]

Of the 16 members who formed the presbytery of Greenock, 12 disassociated from the Established Church. Between 1844–76, 10 new churches were founded in Greenock. By 1851 in Greenock, the number of members of the Free Church was 9,174, while 4,267 belonged to the Established Church.[6]

In Port Glasgow, many ministers gave up everything for the sake of conscience. This disastrously affected the Church of Scotland in that area, which could not procure new ministers. The town minister, James Morrison, brought nearly all his congregation to the Free Church after the disruption. In Newark, the minister came out with a number of his followers and founded the Hamilton Congregation of the Free Church. Kilmacolm's Free Church gained almost equal strength with the Established Church after the Disruption.

Many of these churches initially faced various problems, particularly financial difficulties. Issues of accommodation forced many of them to hold services in nearby graveyards. In many places, benevolent men helped the new church financially to erect a church in, for example, Greenock and Port Glasgow. In Port Glasgow, Captain Hamilton, a retired shipowner, bequeathed to the church his house for a manse and a sum of £2,580 for building the church.

3.1.2 The Contribution of the Free Church to Education in Scotland and Renfrewshire

From its inception, the Free Church has maintained an ever-increasing share in Scotland's educational sphere. The church's success all over Scotland was phenomenal. It attracted many of the most brilliant teachers, but the Established Church took harsh action against the teachers who changed their allegiance. Many were dismissed immediately in 1843, while others in parish schools received a notice of six months.

After six months, it was found that 360 teachers drawn from the parish, Assembly, Sessional, and other types of Established Church schools had joined the new church.[7] The teachers who joined the Free Church took an even more significant risk than the ministers because they had no assurance of employment. "Schools be opened," said Professor Welsh, "to afford a suitable sphere of occupation for parochial, still more for private teachers of schools who were threatened with deprivation of their present office on account of the opinion upon the Church question." At first there was some hesitation as religious teaching in parish schools was considered satisfactory. Still, it was decided that the church would not rest, "until by the side of every Free Church there was planted a Free Church school."[8]

Though the church started the task of educating the rural people with great enthusiasm, this strained its resources. D.J. Withrington, in his article, "The Free Church Education Scheme, 1843–50," points out that the efforts of the church proved that voluntary activity was not enough to meet the educational needs of the 1850s.

Many other historians share his views that the government's schemes to aid teachers in 1846 saved it from collapse. After some hesitation, the Free Church Assembly had agreed by a "deceptive"[9] but large majority to accept government aid conditioned by compulsory inspection. The government would supplement the salary of a certificated teacher, which should be between £30–£35. It also included grants for assistant and pupil-teachers.

In 1846, the new convenor of the Church Education Committee, Dr. Robert Candlish, argued that the Free Church schools would be successful if they reached a high standard and offered teachers a reasonable salary. In 1850, the church had 60 thousand pupils in subsidized schools and 14 thousand in others. The "standard came to be recognized as the highest in the county."[10]

There was no hard and fast rule regarding the denomination of the scholars. Many scholars were drawn from other churches, including the Catholics and Episcopalians. "We do not plant our schools as nurseries of the Free Church," said Dr. Candlish in his statement to the Education Commission in 1865, "nor do we ask our teachers to make proselytes of the pupils. Our schools are really as simply and purely elementary schools for good elementary education to the young as were the best parish schools before the disruption."[11]

The Free Church, despite the fears that it would lead to teaching contrary to the Christian faith, was in favor of ending the confessional tests of the teachers. Pressure from Free and United Presbyterian (U.P.) churches ensured that the end of the confessional tests for schoolmasters could be achieved if only the relationship between the Church of Scotland and parish schools could be relaxed. For years, denominational rivalry frustrated this. The 1854 bill for reforming the education system, put forward by Mr. Moncrieff, the Lord Advocate and an elder of the Free Church, was defeated in Parliament. Ultimately, an act was passed in 1861, which ended the connection between the Established Church and parish schools.

The 1861 Act did not end the involvement of the Free Church in education, but the number of schools under its control fell as it ended the exclusion of the Free Church teachers from the parish schools. There remained no primary difference between the parish and Free Church schools.[12] Nevertheless, the church continued to support its schools and retained complete control of them. Between 1864–7, a Royal Commission was appointed to enquire into the educational conditions in Scotland. The report of the Commission in 1867 was received favorably by the U.P. and Free Church with some reservation on the latter's part about the security of religious instructions. The 1872 Act gave effect to the findings of the Commission. That year, the Free Church had 462 government aided schools, compared to 712 in 1851. Many schools were transferred to the School Board, and by 1886, only 39 schools remained under the church. The teachers' training colleges remained under the church. In 1879, the Free Church opened another training school in Aberdeen for women, as did the Church of Scotland. The Glasgow and Edinburgh training schools were established after Disruption in 1845–46 when David Stow and Oliphant seceded from the Free Church along with all their staff and pupils.[13]

As elsewhere in Scotland, the Free Church played an essential role in Renfrewshire. Schools were being erected in the newly formed churches. Altogether, 16 schools were opened by the 1860s. Even then, in Mearns, Lochwinnoch, and Kilmacolm, the church failed to have any school. In Eastwood, Eaglesham, and Inchinnan, there was no church and no school.

Though evidence on the number of teachers transferring to the Free Church all over Scotland is available, it is difficult to estimate the total number who did so in Renfrewshire. It was probably quite substantial in the burghs. For example, in Greenock, there were seven teachers in two schools and two teachers for the Renfrew school.

Financial difficulties that led to the acceptance of government grants conditioned by inspection of the schools were persistent in the Renfrewshire area. Even when the privy council (P.C) grants were available from 1847, the financial difficulties of the church did not end. There was little endowment available, and the congregation had to pay the teachers' salaries and provide a sufficient sum to obtain the government grant. Moreover, the buildings were to be built spaciously and commodiously if the grant was to be received. It was probably for financial reasons that the church could not erect a school in all the parts of the county where it had a church.

Most of the Free Church schools obtained government grants in the 1860s. Of the 16 schools in the county, nine were receiving grants for certificated teachers. Six of the same schools had grants for pupil-teachers. Besides these, one school in Port Glasgow and one in Renfrew were under government grant. Whether it was for certificated teachers is not known. With the high annual grant amount, it could be argued that the grant was for a certificated teacher. Except for one in Paisley, no other school enjoyed an endowment, but all of them received some donations, subscriptions, and collections in places of worship. The total sum given by the privy council to churches in Renfrewshire between 1833 and 1855 is shown in Table XXIV. Thus, though the Free Church schools were established after 1843, 15 schools received half the grants received by the Established Church schools, making the share more or less proportional. The return of 1854–56 showed that the grant the Committee of Council paid to six Free Church schools amounted to £803- 4s-2¼d.[14]

Table XXIV:
Total sum given by the P.C in Renfrewshire between 1833–55 to different churches

Name of the church	Amount of the grant
Established Church	£858-12s-10d.
Free Church	£331-18s-4d.
Roman Catholic Church	£21-31s-4d.
Episcopal church	£110-10s.

Source: PP 1854/5 xii, 316. The return shows the total amount of education grants from the P.C. to each county in Scotland from 1833 to 1855, distinguishing the object of the grant and the religious denomination to which it was paid. 71.

Thus, the schools under the Free Church obtained more and more certificated teachers to earn grants. M. Monies[15] argued that the teachers of the Free Church schools should have been efficient as they were not appointed on an *ad vitam aut culpam* basis. Instead, they had to satisfy the congregational board, so the schools obtained a satisfactory standard but at a tremendous financial cost.

In 1862–65, there were nine schools in Renfrewshire with 842 scholars and 11 teachers, excluding Paisley and Greenock, which formed 8.4% of the total scholars on roll. The contribution of the church was better in Greenock than in Paisley, where in 1854, two schools with 579 scholars formed 12% of the total students, which was higher than the Established Church schools. At Paisley in the same year, the number of scholars in four Free Church schools was 351, 7% of the children at school and less than the percentage of the Established Church.[16] However, the number must have increased rapidly in Paisley after 1854 as by 1865, in Free South Church schools alone, there were 574 pupils, more than the total of all four schools in 1854.[17]

From the evidence of different sources, it is clear that the Free Church in Renfrewshire was not so vigorous in establishing schools in other parts of the county as in northern Scotland. In most places, the church had its school rival the parish school to draw the children away from the Church of Scotland. For example, in Aberdeen city in 1851, there were 27 Free Church schools as opposed to 13 schools of the Established Church. The Secession was far more vital in the north, establishing a more significant number of schools. In Renfrewshire, the church had failed to erect schools in seven parishes out of 13, including the parishes of Eastwood and Kilbarchan, which had a high total of 1663 and 670 scholars, respectively. The reason for this might have been financial difficulties. However, the church founded schools in some of the most populated centers: Neilston, Paisley, Greenock, Port Glasgow, Cathcart, and Renfrew (Table XXV).

Table XXV:

The number of Free Church and total schools in the parishes and burghs of the county in 1854 and 1856

Name of the parish and burgh	Free Church school	Total schools
Cathcart	1	3
Erskine	1	3
Greenock (burgh) a	2	29
Gourock	1	2
Houston & Killellan	1	7
Inverkip	1	2
Neilston	1	17
Paisley (burgh) a	4*	52

Name of the parish and burgh	Free Church school	Total schools
Port Glasgow (burgh)	2	10
Renfrew (burgh)	1	5
a) 1854 data	15	80

*Another school was erected by the Church in Paisley in 1859. Out of the Harvey Bequest, which amounted to £500, Mr. Harvey was a brewer of Paisley. Source: PP. 1867 xxvi 212–17.

The contribution of the church towards the education of the children was very significant in some parishes, where it had one school out of a total of two or three schools. The number of schools run by the church might seem small, but considering that these were established after 1843, 16 out of 80 schools by 1865 in those areas is quite a good achievement.

It is difficult to assess the role played by the Free Church in improving educational standards, but comparing the number of scholars in the parish and Free Church schools might throw some light on the question (Table XXVI). Almost equal numbers of students were in the Free Church and parish schools. In some areas, more scholars were studying in these schools than in the parish school. The role played by this church in some burghs was also no less remarkable (Table XXVII).

Table XXVI:

Number of scholars in Free Church and parish schools in Towns in some (areas) of Scotland in 1865

Name of the parish	Number of scholars in	
	Free Church school	Parish school
Cathcart	62	130
Erskine	51	93
Houston & Killellan	102	66
Inverkip	67	141
Gourock	159	69

Name of the parish	Number of scholars in	
	Free Church school	Parish school
Neilston	50	237
Total	491	736

Source: PP. 1867 xxvi, 212-17.

Table XXVII:

The number of scholars in Free Church and burgh schools in Renfrewshire, in 1865–67

Name of the burgh	Number of scholars			
	Free Church school		Burgh school	
	No. of schools	Scholars	No. of schools	Scholars
Port Glasgow	2	262	1	56
Renfrew	1	109	2	438
Paisley	1	579	1	500
Total	4	950	4	994

Source: Ibid.-212. Note: No comparison of other Free Church schools of Paisley and Greenock could be made for lack of data for 1865–67.

A study of Ayrshire, Renfrewshire, and Stirlingshire reveals that the Free Church was more active in establishing schools in Ayrshire (Table XXVIII). The percentage of certificated teachers was higher in Stirlingshire (Table XXIX). Still, the percentage of scholars in these schools out of the total children in the whole county was more or less similar (Table XXX), with attendance showing a better record in Renfrewshire (Table XXXI). So, the contribution of the church was no less significant in Renfrewshire.

Table XXVIII:
Number of Free Church schools in Stirlingshire, Ayrshire, and Renfrewshire in the 1860s

Name of county	Free Church schools	Total schools	%
Ayrshire	29	249	12
Renfrewshire	16	195	8
Stirlingshire	11	165	7

Source: PP 1867 xxvi (3845V), PP 1854 /ix, 572, A. Bain, op. cit., 147, W. Boyd, op. cit. 136.

Table XXIX:
No. of Free Church schools receiving grants for certificated teachers in Ayrshire, Renfrewshire, and Stirlingshire in 1861

County	No. receiving the grant	Total schools	%
Ayrshire	20	29	69
Renfrewshire	9	16	56
Stirlingshire	10	11	91

Source: PP 1863 xlvi 100–103.

3.2 The Role Played by the Catholic Church in Education

3.2.1 Introduction

Till the last decade of the 18th century in Scotland, the Roman Catholic Church was a declining minority. In the Hebrides, Aberdeen, and Banffshire, there were some native Catholics, but in the south of the Highlands, there were few. With the coming of the Industrial Revolution, demand for cheap labor in the cotton mills brought some Catholics from the northeast and Isles to the Lanarkshire and Renfrewshire areas. But a large number of them arrived from Ireland. During the 1830s and 1840s, the number of Catholics in the Clyde valley rose considerably.[18]

Table XXX:
Percentage of children studying in Free Church schools in Ayrshire, Renfrewshire, and Stirlingshire

County	Year	No. of scholars in Free Church schools	Total scholars	%
Ayrshire	1865	3,180	31,739	10
Renfrewshire (outside Paisley and Greenock)	1862–5	842	10,019	8.4
Renfrewshire (Paisley and Greenock)	1854	930	8,401	11.1
Stirlingshire		1,200	13,731	9

Source: PP 1867 xxvi, 37–50, 212–24.

Table XXXI:
Percentage of Scholars Attending the Free Church Schools in Ayrshire, Renfrewshire, and Stirlingshire

County	No. of attendances	Total Scholars	%
Ayrshire	2, 408A	3,180	77.7
Renfrewshire	671B	842	80.0
Stirlingshire	943	1, 200	78.6

(A) There is no return from the parishes of Kilmarnock, Irvine.

(B) The attendance data is unavailable for a portion of Abbey Paisley, Paisley Burgh, and Greenock.

Source: PP 1867 xxvi, 37, 50, 212–24.

The Great Famine in Ireland contributed immensely to the migration of the Irish to Scotland. It produced a permanent effect in Scotland in the distribution pattern of faith, and the Catholics made this church the fastest-growing church.[19] The Catholics, primarily Irish in origin, were "desperately" poor, occupying the lowest position on the industrial ladder. Their religious differences added to the divisions based on cultural, racial, and economic factors.[20] There was a rapid increase in Catholics in Neilston, Mearns, Kilbarchan, Houston and Killellan, Lochwinnoch, Port Glasgow, Greenock, and Paisley. Catholic churches were erected in some places of the county by the early 19th century. In Greenock, Catholicism was re-established in 1802 by the priest Father Capron, and St. Mary's Church was opened in 1816.[21] St. Lawrence Chapel and Patrick Street Church were opened in 1855 and 1862 respectively. The first Catholic church in Paisley, St. Mirren Chapel, was established in 1808, and St. Margaret's Chapel was erected in 1841, which served the whole area between Paisley and Greenock. St. Joseph's College, a mission school in Kilbarchan, had a small chapel that served as a place of worship for the Catholics under the care of the secular priest of the Howwood village. In Erskine and Gourock, the Chapels were built in the 1860s and 1870s, respectively.[22] The Port Glasgow Catholic priest became a resident in 1846. Before that, the priest of Glasgow supplied the wants of the Catholics. Thus, by the 1870s, the Catholics had established their own church in some parishes and burghs. The priests provided the leadership to raise the immigrants in their desperate struggle from squalor and slump through education to a better life.

3.2.2 The Efforts of the Catholics for Education in Scotland and Renfrewshire

The majority of the Irish who came to Scotland and formed the bulk of the Catholic population, particularly in the west of Scotland, were ordinary laborers. Their poverty forced the families to seek work from their earliest years, and the long work hours left them little leisure to develop intellectual interests. They realized this interest could be developed for their children by promoting the minimum education. At first, their children attended parish and other Church of Scotland schools (besides the few Catholic schools) and withdrew during religious instruction. The General Assembly's Education Committee allowed this relaxation policy from 1829. The Catholic Emancipation Act opened the parish school to Catholic pupils simultaneously (Table XXXII).

Table XXXII:
No. of Catholic children in Free Church and other schools in Scotland 1840s and 1850s

Type of schools	Total pupils	Catholic pupils
Parish	76,493	1,243
Assembly	33,000	1,000
Free Church	48,000	974
SSPCK	91,000	2,898
Total	248,493	6,115

Sources: PP 1865 xvii, (A.C) Mclauchlan, Menzies, PP 1867 xxv (3845) (A.C.I) xix-xx. C.C.M, 1849/50, Gordon and also in J. Scotland, op. cit., 255.

In the 1840s, over 6,000 children all over Scotland attended Protestant schools, while 5,229 attended Catholic schools. A priest in Edinburgh, Father Rigg, always encouraged the children to participate in Presbyterian institutions, "never having found any attempts at proselytism."[23] The immigrants contributed "pennies" to build schools for their children throughout the early nineteenth century. For this, a "second collection" was gathered from the congregation on Sundays. These efforts, "unsupplemented by any fraction of the £100,000 that the government was granting annually in the forties for school building and inspection, could not sufficiently meet the demands of the rapidly growing community."[24]

The Catholic body of England and Scotland was roused when, in 1847, the Minute of the Education Committee was framed to exclude Catholic schools from grants. Ultimately, they were given a share of the grant upon terms that would not disturb their conscience. The first building grant for Catholic education was made in 1851 when £1,696 was distributed among four schools in England.

Until 1861, grants were awarded, supplementing teachers' salaries and payments to pupil-teachers, with allowance for books and maps. A revised code was introduced in 1862 on the recommendation of the Royal Commission on Education in Scotland (R.C.E.S.) of 1858. This brought together all separate grants into a gross amount to be paid to the manager of the school. This grant was decided considering the number of pupils in attendance, scholars' proficiency, and school management efficiency.[25]

The children were grouped according to their ability into six standards for examination purposes, and the teachers were allowed to divide them according to their discretion. Such a system tempted the teacher to turn his attention from educating the pupil to outwitting the inspectors. For the Catholic teacher anxious to secure for his parish priest the maximum grant to lighten his sore financial need, there was the danger of "harassing his pupil to the edge of endurance."[26] The main drawback of the 1847 Act was that the building grant was offered to the extent of one quarter of the total cost and was not paid where the school was used for church purposes also. A school-cum-chapel building was widespread in mid-19th century Scotland but was excluded from the much needed support from the government. The Roman Catholic and Episcopal churches were against the absorption of their schools by the school boards established after the 1872 Act, and they forfeited the aid drawn from the local rates. As a result, the number of Episcopal schools declined. Despite this, the number of Catholic schools proliferated and remained independent.[27] Grant-aided Catholic schools arose in Scotland at that time—the emergence of a national system of Catholic education dates from the late 19th century. The church had no regular school for teacher training till the 20th century.

Despite the gloomy financial situation and the restriction on the availability of the grant, the efforts of the church towards the education of the Catholic children in Renfrewshire were considerable. Schools were gradually opened. In 1837, there was one Catholic school each in Paisley, Greenock, and Port Glasgow. By 1865 there were altogether 14 schools located in five parishes and three burghs. The following table brings out the significant difference between 1837 and 1865. (Table XXXIII).

Table XXXIII:

No. of scholars in Catholic schools in Renfrewshire between 1837, 1854, and 1865

Name of the parish and burgh	1837		1854		1865	
	No. of schools	No. of scholars	No. of schools	No. of scholars	No. of schools	No. of scholars
Abbey Paisley	-	-	-	-	3	186
Eastwood	-	-	-	-	1	178
Greenock (burgh)	1	110	2*	250	-	-
Kilbarchan	-	-	-	-	1	67
Mearns	-	-	-	-	2	76
Neilston	-	-	-	-	2	238
Paisley	1	90	1	130	-	-
Port Glasgow	1	60	-	-	1	272
Total	3	260	3	380	10	1,017

*Another school in Greenock was erected in 1859. So in all, 14 schools in the coun-ty. Sources: PP 1841 xix, 653–83, PP 1854 lix, 512, PP 1862 xiii, 67, PP 1867 xxvi, 212–17.3.9.16.

There was an increase in the number of Catholic scholars in the county. However, it should be remembered that their population was also increasing rapidly during this period. Although the exact figure of the Catholic population cannot be given for all the parishes, some information can be produced for Paisley, Greenock, Port Glasgow, and Neilston. One exciting feature of Paisley was a decrease in the number of Catholic children because of the out movement of the younger generation in the 1850s due to the trade depression (Table XXXV). Thus, while the number of children decreased, the overall number of scholars increased as the parents were more interested in sending their children to school.

Table XXXIV:

Catholic population and pupils in Renfrewshire between the 1830s and 1870s

Name of parish/burgh	1841 population	No. of scholars in 1837	1861 population	No. scholars in 1865	% increase in population	% increase in no. of scholars
Paisley	5,124	90	5,439 (1851)	130 (1854)	6.14	44.4
Port Glasgow	835	60	2,431	272	191.14	353.33
Neilston	1,061 (1836)		3,000	238	182.75	

Sources: PP 1841 xix, 653–83, PP 1854 lix, 512, PP 1867 xxv, 212–17, J. Handley, op. cit., 50–51, Dr. Pride, op. cit., and Census of Scotland 1871, Vol II.

Table XXXV:

Percentage of changes in number in each group in Paisley between 1841 and 1851

Age group	% change
5–9	-1
10–14	-11
15–19	-11

Source: Table 4.6, Brenda E. A. Collins, op. cit., 160.

A comparison with Lanarkshire (where there was a large number of Catholics) reveals that the efforts of the Catholics in Renfrewshire for educational purposes were more significant than in Lanarkshire, as far as the number of pupils and schools were concerned in the 1860s (Table XXXVI). Many children were also attending other types of schools besides the Catholic church schools, especially in parishes where no such schools existed (Table XXXVII).

Table XXXVI:
Percentage of Catholic pupils out of the total population in 1854–1865 in Lanarkshire and Renfrewshire

County	Catholic population in 1861	No. of pupils in 1865	%
Lanarkshire	93,394	1,349 (1)	1.5
Renfrewshire	24,955	1,397 (2)	5.6

(1) There were fourteen schools in the county, and one school did not give returns as the school was closed/or on holiday.

(2) For convenience, the no. of Catholic scholars o/ Greenock and Paisley of 1854 is included with those of 1865 for the whole county.

Source: (1) Census of Scotland 1861, Vol. II.

(2) PP 1867 xxvi.

Table XXXVI:
Number of Catholic pupils in other schools in 1865

Name of the parish	Number of scholars
Cathcart, Eaglesham, Erskine, Houston and Killellan, Inchinnan, Inverkip, Gourock, Lochwinnoch, and Renfrew	198
Abbey Paisley	20

Name of the parish	Number of scholars
Eastwood	51
Port Glasgow	16
Mearns	16
Total	301

Note: *No definite figure of Catholic scholars for Abbey Paisley except Johnstone, Paisley burgh, and Greenock could be given as there was no mention of the denomination of the pupil in 1854 or 1862 return.*

Source: *PP 1867 xxvi 212–17.*

The problem of non-attendance was acute in these schools. Due to a lack of information, it is impossible to determine the exact percentage of actual school attendance in 1837. In 1865, in Eastwood, Neilston, Kilbarchan, Port Glasgow, and Johnstone of Abbey Paisley, 501 scholars out of 911 attended school at a particular period of the year. Whether these 501 were all Catholics is not known. They formed 55% of the total Catholic pupils and 6.95% of the total pupils in the county (excluding Paisley and Greenock). The absenteeism problem was more prominent in these schools than other church schools.[28] The attendance was worse in Lanarkshire (XXXVIII).

Table XXXVI:

% of non-attendance out of the total scholars in Catholic schools in Renfrewshire and Lanarkshire in 1865

Name of the county	No. of non-attendances	Total scholars	%
Lanarkshire*	956	1349	71.00
Renfrewshire	501	911	55.00

*There was no return from a school that was closed/or on holiday. Source: PP 1867 xxvi, 212–17.

The cause of absenteeism was probably because the children had to work to augment the family income. Children were employed in increasing numbers in textile (non-handweaving) works in textile areas. The following table indicates the number of children employed in Paisley among the Irish population (Table XXXIX).

Table XXXVI:
Percentage of selected age groups of children in textile employment (non-handweaving), children of the household head only Paisley sample 1851, number in brackets

Age group	Irish migrants	Scots migrants	Non-migrants
9–10	12(6)	6(2)	13 (3)
12–13	53(26)	28(8)	37(13)
13–14	60(31)	39(10)	64(14)

Source: Table 7.8, B.E.A. Collins, op. cit., 161.

There were also opportunities for children to work in printwork. In several cases, the reason for sending children to work was the inability to pay school fees. A great deal of the print field boys at Busby (near Paisley) were of Irish parents, many of whom were at the cotton mills and who were put to the printfield to "keep them out of the road."[29]

The fees in Catholic schools were low, ranging from 1d a week in the lowest standard to 3/4d in the highest. Pupils who could not afford the fees were taught gratuitously, the cost was defrayed by the parish society of St. Vincent de Paul, or the fees were raised by charity balls, concerts, bazaars, and voluntary subscriptions. In Greenock in 1854, 110 out of 130 were taught gratuitously. This throws light on the economic condition of their parents. Despite such outside help, the problem of absenteeism remained very acute.

There was also the half-time system. The half-timers had to be at least eleven years of age and beyond the third standard, though sometimes nine-year-old children were accepted. They spent alternate weeks attending school for two to three days and had to work during the rest of the week. The inspectors did not make allowances for them, and the teachers burdened them with double the amount of homework assigned to the rest. This was torture to them; apparently, they often sank exhausted into sleep, even during school time. In 1837, Sunday school was held in all the schools so children could attend classes when they were working full-time. Thus, the efforts of the church to spread education were handicapped due to the poverty of its followers.

Qualitative aspects of these schools have to be based on indirect information. Out of eight schools in five parishes and Port Glasgow in 1865, four received government grants, with Barrhead school in Neilston obtaining the highest grant of £69-10s.[30] Some of them probably had been getting grants for certificated or pupil-teachers as the grants were relatively high. One school in Abbey Paisley [other than those four] received a grant for certificated teachers in 1860. Assuming that the government grant was linked with inspection, these five schools in Renfrewshire had attained a comparable standard with other schools. However, it is relevant to mention here that a government grant was subject to a certain amount of money to be raised for school building. The Irish were poor, so they could not raise the required amount to receive a grant. Probably for this reason, the church received only £21-13-4d in the 1850s. Hence, being non-recipients of grants does not necessarily prove that these schools have poor standards. However, according to J. Scotland, the standard in Catholic schools was as poor as in Episcopal schools because many of the pupils were children of illiterate Irish peasants. The teachers' salaries in these schools were low, £75-12s a year for a certificated teacher and £51-5s for a non-certificated teacher. Another problem was the lack of teacher training facilities in Scotland. In the 1850s, there were two colleges for males in Dublin and Hammersmith, and for females, there was one in Derby. It was difficult for a poor Scottish youth to attend them. So, the number of certificated teachers remained low in Scotland till the end of the 19th century.[31] In 1837, no more than the three Rs, reading, writing, and arithmetic, were taught in the Catholic schools in Renfrewshire.

3.3 The Role Played by the Episcopal Church in Education

The recovery of the Episcopal church in Scotland began slowly in 1792. The reasons were the increasing rate of Anglicization of the upper class in 19th-century Scotland and the education of their sons at English public schools. Particularly in Edinburgh, the appeal of the doctrine and liturgy of the church was very attractive to the educated class. But in the west of Scotland, the influence of the church was weak. The rising middle class preferred Free and U.P. Churches in Glasgow, Paisley, and Greenock. Later, however, the Anglican church attracted some of the commercial and industrial magnates. The church also had a handful of followers among the poorest Irish immigrants, besides the traditional Episcopalians and some of the newly rich.

Until the 1830s, there were only six or seven Episcopal congregations in Glasgow and southwest Scotland. Many churches were built during the forties and fifties, and by the 1870s, there were some forty to fifty in the Diocese of Glasgow and Galloway. The Scottish Episcopal Church Society was the primary source of finance for this rapid growth. Rev. Dr. Gordon, minister of St. Andrew-by-the-Green in Glasgow, expressed in a pastoral letter read in the church in 1868, "During the last twenty years dioceses have progressed more than Glasgow, and there is scarcely a town on either side of the river, where the Episcopal Church cannot be seen rearing its cross aloft, where 60 years ago, there was none."[32]

In Renfrewshire, the Anglican Church had a foothold in Greenock, Port Glasgow, Paisley, and Gourock. The revival of the church began in Greenock in 1823. Sir Michael Stewart granted aground on a small feu duty, and St. John's Church was erected in 1824. The churches established at Gourock and Port Glasgow were originally started as missions under St. John's. In the late nineteenth century, there were two missions in Greenock, St. Stephen's at Candyske and St. John's at Bank Street.[33]

In Scotland, as in the case of the other churches, the connection between the Episcopal church and education was very close. In 1841, the Church Society financed 13 schools in Glasgow, Paisley, and the Highlands with 1,800 children on roll. Donations came from all over Scotland, England, Ireland, and India to funds set up in the 1838 Synod. Stipends were given to Episcopalian masters, and poor students received books. There was an increase in the number of schools from 37 in 1849 to 120 in 1859 under the inspection of the Society in Scotland. Like other church schools, these were also open to children of different denominations. Two thousand out of six thousand pupils in 74 schools surveyed by the church schools declined after 1872 when School Boards were established. The church opposed the absorption of her schools by the Boards and forfeited the aid from the local rates. The Act of 1872 provided that schools not transferred to the School Board's control could receive grants by attaining a high efficiency standard. In 1872, there were 87 Episcopalian schools receiving grants in Scotland retaining independence, but the number dropped to 73 in 1880.

In 1837, there was only one Anglican Church school in Renfrewshire at Greenock. It was established in 1834 as a day and infant school with 72 pupils. The number of schools increased to five in 1854, with three in Greenock and one in Paisley and Port Glasgow. These schools were erected in the late 1840s. (Table XL).

Table XL:

No. of Episcopal Church schools in Renfrewshire in 1837, 1854, and 1865

Name of burgh	No. of schools	No. of scholars	No. of schools	Year	No. of scholars
Greenock	1	72	3	1854	120
Paisley	-	-	1	1854	69
Port Glasgow	-	-	1	1865	138

Sources: PP 1841 xix, 653–83, PP 1854; lix, 512, PP 1867 xxvi 212–17.

As in the rest of Scotland, these schools were not exclusive to the Episcopalians. Figures are available only for the Port Glasgow School; out of 138, only 56 Episcopalians and others belonged to different denominations. Similarly, some children belonging to the church were in non-Episcopal schools. The number was 39 in each county, excluding Paisley and Greenock.

The absenteeism problem in these schools was similar to the other schools in the county. Subscriptions, donations, and little endowments in 1860 ran these schools. All the schools, except one each in Paisley and Greenock, received government grants. The Port Glasgow School received grants for certificated teachers.[34] The percentage of Episcopal schools enjoying government grants was only second to Free Church schools (Table XLI).

Table XLI:
Grants received by schools under different churches in Renfrewshire in 1865

Name of the Church	No. of schools receiving grants	Total schools	%
E. Church	23	48	49
Free Church	11	16	69
Catholic Church	5	14	36
Episcopal	3	5	60

Source: PP 1863 xlvi 101, PP 1867 xxvi, 212–17.

Besides reading, writing, and arithmetic, tables of weights, measuring, geography, and religious studies were followed by the Greenock Episcopal School in 1837. This school was inspected by the Episcopal minister and others who were friendly to it during that period. In the 1840s, these schools were inspected by inspectors belonging to the church. However, the proportion of the children under the Episcopal church was very small and contributed in a limited way to the education of the children in the county.

3.4 Conclusion

The Free, Catholic, and Episcopal churches played their due part in the education of the children in the county. The Disruption increased the number of schools. By 1865, sixteen new schools had been erected by the Free Church. The Free Church could not supply schools in every parish. Still, it erected schools in larger parishes and towns where there was a need for educational provision, so their contribution was significant. Seven percent of scholars attended these schools in Paisley, and at Greenock, such schools were educating 12% of the pupils in 1854. Slightly more than 8% of the scholars were on the roll in Free Church schools in 1862–65 in the county outside Paisley and Greenock.[35] These were some of the best schools in the county, and the proportion of grants they received was higher than any other schools.

The Catholic church tried its best to provide education for the poor inhabitants belonging to the church. At first, there was not much help from the government, and the church was instructing several children through collection and subscriptions. Sometimes, the teacher's salary was paid through a subscription, and some children were offered free instruction. There was a rise in the number of children attending Catholic schools in proportion to the expansion of the Catholic population. But there was also an acute problem of absenteeism as children had to work to augment the family income and could not attend school despite the Factory Acts and low fees in these schools. The schools that belonged to this church were educating 2.5% of the scholars in Paisley and 8% of the pupils in Greenock in 1854. The total number of students in these schools in Abbey Paisley in 1861 was 17% of the scholars, while in the county other than these three places, the percentage of scholars in these schools was 10% in 1865.

The Episcopal church schools were instructing a small number of children in the county, 4% in Greenock, 1.35% in Paisley, and 1.32% in other parts of the county in 1865. Sunday schools were held in all these different types of church schools, which enabled some more children to gain literacy.

Despite the churches' efforts, a considerable number of children in the county were not on any school roll. These religious bodies were unable to meet the expanding population's education demands. A lack of central control and non-attendance indicated the absence of compulsion. Attendance was irregular, and the churches could not do anything about the absenteeism. Thus, although the religious bodies had responsibly performed their duties, central control was needed. There remained a gap in the educational provision in the county, which schools of other secular bodies filled.

Chapter 4: The Secular Efforts in Education in Renfrewshire

4.1 The Role of the State

From the 17th century onwards, there were occasional instances of state intervention in Scottish education. However, during the 19th century, the state significantly intensified its involvement in the educational landscape. The Education Acts of 1803, 1838, and 1861 were formulated to enhance the educational infrastructure within parishes and burghs. These acts expanded the authority of local bodies, ultimately culminating in complete state control through the Act of 1872. The legislative measures of the 19th century not only curtailed the influence of the Established Church but also facilitated grants for construction projects across various denominational bodies.

The initial public funding for education construction occurred in 1833 when the Scottish government granted £20,000. This grant, renewed annually by the C.C.E[1]. In 1839, a Special Committee of the Council, was appointed to consider matters in education with Sir Kay Shuttleworth as its Permanent Secretary. It made grants for the inspection of schools and supplemented the works of the subscribers in building schools through religious and other organizations. In Scotland, the first aid was given in establishing teachers' training colleges. Until 1846, the grants were confined to supplement the building of a school and the purchase of books and equipment.

From 1846 onward, grants were provided to increase the salaries of teachers who successfully passed a certification examination. Before this grant was introduced, there was already a system in place for training teachers. In Glasgow, David Stow, originally from Paisley, had been providing instruction to teachers since 1827 at Drygate. The Glasgow Education Society later took over this initiative. In 1841, the E.E.C. assumed control of this institution with the assistance of a government grant. The first plan for a training school by the Established Church was outlined by a subcommittee in 1834. By 1837, the sessional school of Edinburgh became the assembly's normal seminary. Following the Disruption, the Free Church established teachers' training colleges in Glasgow and Edinburgh. Even after the control of the churches on the schools was lifted in 1872, the training of teachers remained under the purview of the churches. Although the state did not establish training schools, it supported teacher training by supplementing the salaries of certified teachers and providing grants for the construction of training schools.

In July 1846, the whig government decided to implement grants for pupil-teachers, a system outlined in Kay Shuttleworth's Minute on August 26, 1846. These pupil-teachers typically apprenticed for five years, instruct a class, and receive guidance from the lead teacher before or after regular school hours. The system proved beneficial, as many pupil-teachers later enrolled in training colleges. In 1862, all the various grants for construction, certified teachers, and pupil-teachers were amalgamated into a single lump sum to be paid to the school management. A grant of four shillings per scholar was awarded to those who attended more than 200 days a year, with an additional eight shillings given after an examination on the three

Rs: reading, writing, and arithmetic; 2/8d. was deducted for each failure. In evening school, scholars could earn 5/- through examination attendance at 24 meetings.[4]

To ensure the judicious use of grant funds, inspectors were appointed. Initially, David Stow was approached for the position, followed by J. Gordon, the Secretary of E.C.C. Ultimately, John Gibson, the English master at Madras College in St. Andrews, was appointed in July 1840. After the Disruption, he aligned with the Free Church and resumed inspecting Free Church schools from 1844 onwards. Concurrently, in 1844, J. Gordon became the inspector for visiting Church of Scotland schools, including parish schools. Starting in the early 1850s, Thomas Wilkinson visited Episcopal schools, while Mr. S.N. Stokes oversaw Catholic institutions in both England and Scotland.[5] The allocation of grants hinged on the reports provided by these inspectors, leading to a centralized control system. They examined schools receiving grants, compiled reports, and also conducted investigations into the state of education in specific districts upon request.

Yearly, the inspectors provided reports on the arrangement of desks, the use of apparatus and books, school organization, instructional methods, and the student's achievements. Starting in the 1860s, they began examining pupils organized into six standards selected by the teachers. These examinations often had a significant attendance of parents. Inspectors also visited schools that did not receive grants but were open to state officials. They tactfully worked to address organizational issues by leveraging financial pressure, threatening to withhold grants if necessary. The number of schools inspected in Scotland increased, with a third of all schools being inspected by the 1860s. Despite having denominational roots, state inspection proved highly successful in Scotland. The Presbyterian examination, although now conducted more carefully, had lost credibility. Recognizing the advantages of state inspection over its system, the Church of Scotland and its teachers acknowledged the stimulus it provided.[6]

In Renfrewshire, the state played a significant role in fostering education development through the grant system. Between 1833 and 1855, the Privy Council provided grants to various denominations. The specific amounts of these grants are detailed in the following table (Table XLII).

Table XLII:
Grants to schools from 1833-55 under different denominations in Renfrewshire

Name of the church	Grants in augmentation of the salaries of the schoolmasters and mistresses	Grants in stipends to pupil-teacher and gratuities for special instructions	Grants for building improvements enlargement and fixation	Grants for school books and maps	Total
E. Church	£437-19-3	£1,159-18-4	£3,335-0-0	£32-5-2¾	£4,965-3-2¾
F. Church	£243-7-6	£361-0-0	£793-0-0	£14-9s	£1,441-16-7
Episcopal	-	£8-6-8	£80-0-0	-	£88-6-8
Total					£6,495-6-5¾

Source: PP 1854/5, xii, Re111rn showing the total amount of educational grants from! he Privy Council to each county in Scotland from 1833–55, describing 1he object of the grant, and religious denomination to which it was paid-316.

During this period, substantial grants were allocated to various churches, significantly contributing to the growth of the number of schools. This financial support also facilitated notable improvements in school infrastructure. Providing grants contingent on inspection motivated heritors in certain county parishes to enhance their schools. By the 1860s, nine out of thirteen parish schools were benefiting from grants. The augmentation of teachers' salaries, stipends for pupil-teachers, and building grants played a crucial role in helping the Free Church meet the educational demands of the county. Beyond church schools, other educational institutions experienced improvement, as indicated by the steady increase in grant amounts recorded in the returns of C.C.E. (Table XLIII).

Table XLIII:

Amount of grant paid by C.C.E. to schools in Renfrew- shire in 1854, 1855, 1856

Year	No. of schools	Amount of grant
1854	20	£637-4s-1.1/2d
1855	26	£820-17s-4.1/4d
1856	33	£1114 -5s -8d
Total		£2572-7s-1.3/4d

Source: PP 1857/8 xivi-40, *Return for the years 1854, 1855, and 1856 respectively, of names of the parish in each county in Scotland within whose bounds any school is situated in respect of which any money has been paid under the authority of the Committee of Council on Education.*

The inspectors' reports likely conveyed positive feedback, evident in the increased number of grants. A significant portion of these grants was allocated to Paisley Burgh, leading to a rapid rise in the number of schools in the town by the 1850s. A total of 38 schools in the county received grants during this period. Among them, 5 schools that were on grants in previous years were not granted in 1856, highlighting that school inspection was not a routine process, and schools could be downgraded. In

Renfrewshire in 1860, £2,676-8s-8d was distributed to 46 schools for certificated teachers, assistant teachers, pupil-teachers, and gratuities to masters and mistresses. By 1861, the number of schools increased to 50, with grants raised to £2,927. Six were new schools, and some older schools no longer received grants. In 1864, the C.C.E. provided annual grants to 17 new schools, increasing the total number to 64, while three older schools lost their grants. Comparing these figures with Stirlingshire and Ayrshire underscores the extent of state aid to schools in Renfrewshire (Table XLIV).

Table XLIV:
The total amount of grant given to schools in Ayrshire, Renfrewshire, Stirlingshire, and Scotland as a whole by C.C.E. in 1864 and 1867

Name of the county	No. of schools receiving grant	Total schools	Amount of grant	% of schools receiving grant
Ayrshire	97	246	£5,625-0-0d	39.43
Renfrewshire	64	195	£3,300-0-0d*	32.82
Stirlingshire	49	165	£2,212-19-10d	29.70
Scotland	1,440	-	£71,031-16-0d**	-

*Roughly; **out of a total of £152,418-6-1 l. 1/2d.*

Sources: A. Bain, op. cit., 181, PP 1867 xxvi, PP. 1867 xxv. 'Appendix to first Re-port', W. Boyd, op. cit.. 149.

4.2 The Contribution of the Town Councils

4.2.1 Burgh Schools in Scotland and Renfrewshire

While the Church of Scotland played a crucial role in education within Scottish parishes, a secular perspective on education persisted in the burghs from the 16th century. Following the Reformation, control over burgh schools gradually shifted from the church to the municipality. As the councils assumed responsibility for school maintenance, they also asserted their right to patronage. The church retained authority only over overseeing the religious orthodoxy of the masters and the school curriculum. "Acts of Parliament and Assembly consistently reiterated these points" well into the 18th century.[7] Eventually, by the end of the century, the councils had gained complete control over these schools.

Some of these schools accommodated students across all levels, ranging from those acquiring basic knowledge to advanced learners delving into Latin, Grammar, and other complexities. In Renfrewshire, in schools overseen by the councils, students commenced their education at the elementary level. Therefore, it is crucial to examine these burgh schools, as they significantly contributed to both secondary and elementary education. As per the 1867 Commissioner's report, the majority of students attending these schools typically came from the lower and upper middle classes, although a few were from the working classes.[8]

In 1868, Scotland had 58 burgh schools, with 21 partially managed by heritors and others fully operated by councils.[9] The responsibility of constructing school buildings rested on the municipalities. The burgh council financed these expenses from the "Common Good," a comprehensive fund sourced from "land and fishing rents, feu duties, imports on mills and markets, charges for the use of funeral bell and more cloths, and fines for blood and battery."[10] In instances of insufficient funds, a call for voluntary contributions was initiated.

In Renfrewshire, the grammar and mathematical schools in the four burghs did not fall under the council's jurisdiction simultaneously. The Grammar School of Paisley, established in 1586, was the oldest school to come under the governance of the town council. King James IV of Scotland's endowments in 1577 mandated the construction of the school, provision of a salary for the teacher or "precentor," and support for the indigent children of the burgh. By the end of the 19th century, in addition to the grammar school, there was an English school for the church parish, a commercial school for the Middle, and another school for the Low Church parishes, all under the control of the Paisley Council. In 1864, the grammar, High, and Middle Church schools were amalgamated to establish Paisley Grammar School and Academy. The Low Parish School ceased operations in 1867.

As per the NSA, Greenock had two burgh schools. One was the grammar school, offering instruction in Latin, Greek, and French, while the other was the writing mathematical school, focusing on writing, arithmetic, geography, drawing, and mathematics. Between 1855 and 1857, these two schools were merged to form Greenock Academy, overseen by a board of directors. This consolidation was recommended by a committee established in 1847 in response to the demands of the burgh's residents for an inquiry into educational facilities. Notably, an attempt to construct an academy in the late 18th century had failed to materialize.

The Grammar School of Renfrew had a longstanding history, with Queen Anne's Charter of 1703 affirming the charter granted by James VI in 1614, which had converted the hospital into a grammar school. In 1864, this school was merged with another one, built through subscriptions in memory of Mr. Campbell of Blythswood. However, the two schools were subsequently separated again in 1850. In Port Glasgow, the burgh school faced challenges in maintenance. According to Harvey and Sellar, it reasonably fulfilled the functions of an ordinary school but fell short in meeting the requirements of a burgh school.[11]

4.2.2 Power and Duties of the Council

The council had authority over the appointment and dismissal of the master, determining salary, fees, and the subjects to be taught. In some instances, masters were selected following a public examination, as exemplified in Greenock when Mr. Mitchell was appointed from a pool of 15 candidates.[12] Their tenure was subject to the council's pleasure, and they were obligated to provide three months' notice to the magistrates and council before leaving their positions. The council in newspapers typically advertised vacancies for the office of the rector or other masters. On rare occasions, the council permitted the rector to choose a substitute. In 1841, Mr. Hunter of Paisley Grammar School was allowed to find a substitute when he needed to go to Liverpool before his successor was appointed.[13]

The appointment of masters typically followed a lifetime or fault-based tenure, with occasional exceptions. Town council schoolmasters received the highest salaries among the burghs, and the council frequently rewarded masters for their services by granting them positions. In 1832, when Mr. Peddle, the rector of Paisley Grammar School, retired after 35 years of service, the council decided to provide him with a retiring allowance of £42 annually. The council's support extended beyond schools under their direct control, deviating from 17th and 18th-century practices. Particularly in Greenock and Paisley, it often allocated funds to other schoolmasters and mistresses to encourage them, recognizing that the council alone couldn't meet the educational demands of the growing population.

The council had the authority to permit the master to adjust fees whenever they deemed it necessary, sometimes under external pressures to do so. There were instances when the council hesitated to construct a new school building or relocate the school to a more suitable location. In certain cases, the teacher had to independently secure a larger school, after which the council would grant permission for occupation. The annual school examination took place in the presence of the town minister, magistrates, council members, and notable individuals.

The council did not always exert complete control over teachers, who retained the right to refuse compliance with council rules. An instance from August 1833 illustrates this, where a complaint was lodged against Mr. Rankin of Low Parish School for neglecting his duties, specifically for his absence from all sessional meetings for a year and failure to maintain the register. The council referred the matter to the school committee to investigate the parish register and assess his suitability for session clerk and teacher roles. Mr.

Rankin initiated legal action against the council and session for payment related to his specific duties. Although the council defended itself, the matter was unresolved as Mr. Rankin passed away in 1839. In another incident in 1844, the council dismissed Mr. March, the master of Low Parish School, and session clerk, appointing Mr. R. Donald as his replacement. However, in January 1845, Mr. March took possession of the schoolroom, leading to Mr. Donald's resignation. The council took legal measures, but it was not until July that the sheriff substitute granted a warrant for Mr. March's eviction.

4.2.3 Role Played by the Burgh Schools in Renfrewshire

Between 1837 and 1867, there was a noticeable increase in the proportion of children attending burgh schools in Greenock and Renfrew relative to the growth in population. However, in Paisley, there was a decline in this proportion. This shift is likely attributed to a decrease in middle-class children, potentially caused by migration from the town during the Depression. The data on the number of children in Port Glasgow school is only available for 1865 (refer to Tables XLV and XLVI). In 1865, 1,877 children were enrolled in various burgh schools across the county, including Port Glasgow. Unfortunately, the percentage of scholars out of the total number of children attending these schools cannot be determined due to the unavailability of data on total scholars in Paisley and Greenock for 1865.

Table XLV:
Number of pupils in the burgh schools at Paisley, Greenock, and Renfrew in 1837 and 1865

Name of the burgh	1837		1865	
	No. of schools	No. of scholars	No. of schools	No. of scholars
Paisley	4	522	1	500
Greenock	2	220	1	883
Renfrew	1	97	2	438
Total	6	829	4	1,821

Sources: PP 1841 xix, 653–83, PP 1867 xxvi, 217, PP 1867/8 xxix, 119–175.

Attendance at Paisley and Greenock Academies was commendable, with certain departments boasting a perfect 100% attendance, such as the commercial and modern language department in Paisley and the commercial department in Greenock. This high attendance rate was likely influenced by the predominantly upper-middle-class composition of students in these departments, including individuals from manufacturing, banking, and mercantile backgrounds. In contrast, the issue of non-attendance was prevalent in Port Glasgow, where the student body primarily consisted of individuals from the lower-middle class, including shopkeepers and ship captains, with some representation from the impoverished class (refer to Table XLVII). It is important to note that these schools were open to students from all social classes, resulting in a diverse mix of students. Despite the varied social composition, Mr. Fearon, who reported to the English Inquiry Commission in 1868, expressed the view that burgh schools were well-received among poorer parents. This positive reception was attributed to the presence of day schools with extensive elementary departments catering to the educational needs of a broad spectrum of the population.[1]

Table XLVI:

Percentage of increase in number of scholars in burgh schools in comparison to the growth of population in Paisley, Greenock, and Renfrew.

Burgh	Population in 1831	Pupils in 1837	Population in 1861	Pupils in 1865	% of increase in population	% of increase and decrease in no. of scholars
Paisley	31,460	522	1,538	500	.2	4.2 (decrease)
Greenock	27,571	220	3,894	883	59.2	301.4 (increase)
Renfrew	2,833	97	4,684	231	64.1	178.0 (increase)

Sources: Ibid.

Table XLVII:

No. of children attending burgh schools out of the total scholars on roll in 1865

Name of the burgh	No. of pupils attending schools	Total scholars	%
Paisley	459	500	92
Greenock	708	883	80
Renfrew	356	438	81
Port Glasgow	39	56	70
Total	1,562	1,877	88

Sources: PP 1867 xxvi, 216–7, and PP 1867/8 xxix, 119–75.

Co-education was the prevailing norm in these schools. However, in some larger burghs, girls were an exception; there were distinct ladies' colleges in Edinburgh, Glasgow, and

Aberdeen. In places like Inverness, Dundee, and Greenock, girls were segregated into separate classes as they advanced. Conversely, girls were freely allowed to mix in the playground in Dumfries, Hamilton, Paisley, and similar locations. Notably, there was a significant presence of girls in higher classes in Paisley, Greenock, Port Glasgow, and Renfrew. Many of these girls pursued teaching careers, which were highly esteemed during that era. For instance, in Greenock, out of 883 children, 354 were girls, while in Paisley, the number was 196 out of 500.

During the early 19th century, except for Port Glasgow, the burgh schools were primarily focused on classical education. Renfrew's Blythswood testimonial, in particular, gained renown for its emphasis on classical studies, with Latin being a prominent subject until the mid-19th century. Meanwhile, Paisley Academy offered instruction in Greek and French. As the 19th century progressed, mathematics and commerce gained popularity as subjects in these burgh schools. Additionally, the curriculum shifted towards including subjects like history, geography, navigation, and drawing. English reading and spelling were generally proficient in most of these schools. A comprehensive examination by the assistant commissioners in Renfrew, specifically at Blythswood Testimonial, is detailed in Table XLVIII.

Table XLVIII:
Failure and passes among the children in Renfrew Blysthswood Testimonial School in 1867

No. of children above six qualified by 200 Attendance		147	
No. present for examination		94	
Standard I	Passed	No. present	19
		Reading	19
		Writing	19
		Arithmetic	18
Standard II	Passed	No. present	10
		Reading	10
		Writing	10
		Arithmetic	10
Standard III	Passed	No. present	18
		Reading	17
		Writing	17
		Arithmetic	18
Standard IV	Passed	No. present	19
		Reading	19
		Writing	13
		Arithmetic	15

Standard V	Passed	No. present	25
		Reading	25
		Writing	12
		Arithmetic	25
Standard VI	Passed	No. present	3
		Reading	3
		Writing	3
		Arithmetic	3
Total number of passes in reading, arithmetic, and writing		255	

Sources: *PP 1867/8 xxix–121.*

The achievements in reading and arithmetic across all standards showed considerable promise. However, writing posed a challenge, particularly in standards IV and V. Within the academies, a system of organizing children into distinct classes was implemented. Notably, in Greenock, classes were as small as 35 scholars. These classes were structured into departments, each led by separate masters, with a nominal oversight by a rector. The departments included classical studies, modern languages, English, mathematics, commerce, art, drawing, and more. The masters held authoritative roles within their respective departments and played a significant role in the hiring and dismissal of their assistants. The rector, alongside commercial, classical, and English masters, benefitted from the assistance of additional teachers in their academic pursuits.

Given the high competitiveness of these positions, the rector and masters held elevated qualifications. They were typically university graduates or had received training from the Free or

Established Church Normal Training School in Edinburgh or Glasgow. Consequently, the curriculum, class division methods, and teachers' qualifications met the established standards prevalent in burgh schools and academies during that era in Scotland.

4.3 Subscription Schools (Infant, Endowed, Industrial and Factory)

4.3.1 Introduction

In addition to church and burgh schools, another category addressing the educational needs of children consisted of subscription schools. These schools were prevalent in both urban centers and rural areas. An estimate by one of H.M. Inspectors suggested that there were approximately 450 such schools in Scotland in 1857, with 49 located in the southwest region. An example from the 1830s highlights a primitive form of "voluntary subscription" school that thrived in Cathcart. In this setting, villagers collectively provided lessons to all children every evening from eight to ten p.m. Unfortunately, there is no information available about this school in 1865. Some subscription schools were established and maintained through the contributions of a single individual, with support from others in the community. Frequently, an individual donated a schoolhouse or teacher's residence, and the school's financial needs were met through subscriptions. These schools varied in focus, with some primarily dedicated to industrial training and others focused on the education of infant children.

4.3.2 Infant and Endowed Schools

Several subscription schools were categorized as infant schools, and their development steadily advanced from the mid-twenties. These schools primarily served students aged two to six, with some extending their services up to 10 years old following the enforcement of factory acts. Pioneers in establishing such schools included Robert Owen and James Buchanan, who initiated a school at New Lanark in 1816. David Stow played a crucial role in the west of Scotland, founding the Glasgow Infant School Society in 1826 in collaboration with Professor David Welsh. The State played a role in nurturing the growth of infant schools, as evidenced by a minute in 1856. This minute stipulated that grants would be provided to training colleges offering special courses for infant school mistresses. In Renfrewshire, there were two to three such schools in 1865. One of these was associated with a bleachfield and was constructed through subscriptions. Its purpose was to care for the young children of working mothers. The teachers in these schools were either females or males assisted by a female teacher.

During the mid-thirties, a dedicated Infant and Juvenile school emerged in Greenock, specifically catering to the impoverished children of Highland origin. This institution was established through a combination of public subscription and government grant support. In the burghs of Renfrewshire, several schools were founded by philanthropic individuals to provide education for children from less affluent backgrounds, often relying on subscription funding. Noteworthy contributions came from Alan Kerr, an industrialist in Greenock, who constructed schools for the benefit of the community. One such school, established in 1813, aimed to offer affordable elementary education to the children of tradesmen. In the 1840s, it was entrusted to the kirk session. Another industrialist, Thomas Frairie, played a role in founding and financially supporting the construction of various schools. Similar institutions in Paisley featured minimal fees, facilitating the study of children from working-class families. In one of these schools, the lady teacher and assistant provided free instruction for children unable to afford reading lessons. In Renfrew, Mrs. Spiers and Mrs. Campbell each supported a school, both managed by female teachers.[18]

In addition to the previously mentioned schools, this compilation includes endowed schools. In Paisley, Mr. and Mrs. Park, in 1797, bequeathed £1,500 for "erecting, establishing and endowing a charity school in the town of Paisley to be called Hucheson's charity school, for the end and purposes of educating poor orphans or the children of the poor parents residing in the town of Paisley... in reading English and the principles of common religion ..."[19] The school, focusing on reading English and the principles of common religion, commenced operations in 1804. Another endowed school emerged from the contributions of Maxwell and his son James Maxwell in the late 18th century. Yet another school was established according to the deeds of Mr. and Mrs. Corse. The Free Church managed a school from 1859, utilizing the funds from the Harvey Bequest, while other bequests, including the Cochrane Bequest, were allocated for educational purposes in 1849. In Port Glasgow, David Beaton's generous bequest in

1814 amounted to £1,400, dedicated to constructing and establishing a school for the education of poor or orphan children. By 1840, 150 individuals received free instruction, with additional students benefiting from low charges. Meanwhile, Greenock housed a charity school since 1792, funded through public subscriptions. In the parish of Eaglesham, a charity school was sustained using funds from the Rainy endowment.

Benevolent individuals also played a crucial role in advancing secondary education, exemplified by the "John Neilson Institution" in Paisley. Established in 1839 with £18,000 bequeathed by J. Neilson of Nethercommon, the funds were designated:

> to form and endow an institution for educating, clothing, and outfitting, and if necessary, maintaining boys residing within the parliamentary boundary of Paisley for at least three years. This applied to those whose parents had passed away either without leaving sufficient funds for such purposes or who, due to financial constraints, were unable to provide suitable education for their children.[20]

This institution gained significant renown, with its scholars demonstrating successful competition against the Grammar school. In addition to the foundationers, many children received education at affordable fees.

4.3.3 Industrial and Ragged School

Industrial schools provided professional training to both boys and girls. In Renfrewshire in 1865, there were three such schools, with Pollockshaws as a representative example.

Approximately a hundred students were engaged in learning carpentry, tailoring, and shoemaking, receiving both theoretical and practical instruction. In 1859 alone, the students at Pollockshaws produced "40,831 bundles of firewood and 2,221 articles." For girls attending these schools, the curriculum encompassed knitting, sewing, cookery, baking, washing, and scrubbing.[21] This institution received a substantial amount of grants, including an industrial grant of £133, signifying the growing importance of this type of educational facility. The significance of these schools was highlighted in a minute of the C.C.E. in 1846, which defined them as "schools situated in the denser parts of great cities and intended to attract vagrant youths from the streets, providing training to prevent them from engaging in criminal pursuits or becoming accustomed to begging and vagrancy."[22]

Several industrial schools were designated as Female Industrial Schools, emerging in the 19th century to provide education for working-class girls. Historically, female education had been overlooked, with girls often confined to domestic responsibilities, caring for the household and younger siblings.

Female Industrial schools were staffed by female teachers. Mr. Gordon, the Established Church Inspector of one such school, noted in his testimony before the Education Commission, "The entirety of female education, both in literacy and industrial activities, was overseen by female teachers exclusively for female children."[23] The majority of female teachers, upon completing training colleges in the mid-19th century, often found employment in industrial schools. In 1858, for instance, nine out of thirteen graduates from the Established Church training colleges in Glasgow had chosen to work in such schools.

Typically, these schools aimed to train ordinary girls in skills such as sewing, needlework, and religious studies. Some schools also included instruction in reading, writing, and music. In Renfrewshire, there were several such schools, with Eastwood parish alone hosting around four female industrial schools out of the total seven in the entire county in 1865, excluding those in Paisley and Greenock. According to information from the NSA, there were schools in Paisley and Greenock where female teachers focused on providing education in areas such as music and sewing. In Greenock, a Gaelic Female Industrial School was established to cater to girls of Highland origin, funded by the "Gaelic Church and School Accommodation Society" as well as through subscription. Additionally, it was common for the mistress of a female school to be employed to teach sewing in burgh schools, as seen in Paisley.[24]

These industrial schools catered to the most disadvantaged segment of the urban population, with some functioning essentially as reformatories. The exclusively reformatory schools emerged following the enactment of the Youthful Offenders Act in 1854, while the older industrial schools operated under the governance of the Industrial Act of the same year. Their oversight was entrusted to the Home Department in 1860. One reformatory school, established in Paisley, originated from an endowment by Mrs. Elizabeth Kibble of Greenlaw, Paisley. She allocated funds for the "founding and endowing in Paisley an institution to reclaim youthful offenders against the laws."[26] In 1859, when the school opened, there were 14 convicted boys in attendance. In addition to basic education, a tailor and a shoemaker were employed to teach the boys practical skills. According to the director's report in 1865, by the end of that year, 51 boys were on the school's roll. Twenty-nine had been discharged the previous year, with 18 reported to be doing well, four in a doubtful situation, and four having been convicted of crimes again.

The ragged schools, considered a notable offshoot of industrial schools, made their way to Scotland in the early 1840s. This movement was initiated by John Pounds, a disabled cobbler from Portsmouth. The Ragged School Union was established in London in 1844. The first Scottish industrial feeding school, led by Sheriff Watson, opened its doors in Aberdeen in 1841. Initially, these schools did not qualify for privy council grants. However, in the 1860s, the government, through a formal minute, decided to contribute by covering half of the rent for such schools, half of the certified teachers' salaries, and one third of other associated costs. Additionally, a capitation grant was introduced for children provided with food, and instruction, not funded by the treasury. For industrial schools in England, the grant was 5/- per child, while in Scotland, it was 6/6, intended explicitly for vagrant children sent by magistrates to the school.[27]

The inception of the ragged school in Johnstone took place in 1850, established through subscriptions to address the substantial number of destitute and neglected children in the town. The motivation behind its establishment was articulated as addressing the plight of children,

> who having no regular means of living, nor any moral superintendence on the part of parents or relatives, are allowed to grow up in habits of vagrancy and crime, that this class forms the great and increasing source of juvenile delinquency which is the disgrace of our large towns.[28]

The female section of the school was overseen by the ladies of Paisley, who conducted weekly visits and quarterly examinations. The initial report from the directors on February 2, 1850, outlined that the education provided to the children encompassed reading, writing, common arithmetic rules, geography, and music. Girls received instruction in knitting, sewing, and kitchen duties, preparing them for the responsibilities of domestic life. The school aimed to provide half of its training in industrial skills, aiming to socialize unruly, vagrant, and destitute children for integration into an industrial society. In 1856, the school obtained certification as an industrial school, and by 1861, there were 106 pupils engaged in learning reading, 65 in writing, and 39 in arithmetic.

4.3.4 Factory Schools

In Renfrewshire, several factory schools played a role in alleviating the strain on educational resources. Typically constructed by proprietors, some schools were initiated through subscriptions by the workers themselves. An example from 1836 in Lochwinnoch illustrates this collaborative effort, where the owners of a new mill provided a teacher with £30 per year to instruct 60 scholars—30 at 6 p.m. and an additional 60 in the evening at 8 p.m. Beginning in the 1840s, the government displayed a willingness to support the education of factory children through grants and legislation. One challenge faced by works schools was the inadequate attendance of pupils to qualify for a grant. However, in 1864, the C.C.E. introduced provisions for grants to these schools, accommodating pupils who attended part-time. Under this system, children could attend class either half a day or every second day, with the qualifying number of attendances set at 88. Many works and factories adopted this half-time approach. In Johnstone, Renfrewshire, two such schools embraced the half-time system, with children attending both in the forenoon and afternoon in relay shifts. Despite criticism from figures like David Stow, who argued that children couldn't learn effectively in just two hours after "hurrying from a heated factory to a master whose main qualification was incapacity to any other work," this system persisted.[29] As late as 1872, Dr. Middleton, an H.M. Inspector, reported that "half-timers make very little progress," with teachers expressing concerns about their irregularity and attendance.[30] Nevertheless, this system endured until 1872.

Some factory schools in Renfrewshire offered evening and night classes, catering to scholars typically aged between 13 and 20 years. There were also a few children below 13 years who primarily focused on reading and occasionally writing. After a day's work, many pupils faced challenges concentrating on their studies. Some of these schools also conducted Sunday classes.

These factory schools were predominantly situated in Eaglesham, Eastwood, Gourock, Mearns, Kilbarchan, Lochwinnoch, Neilston, and Johnstone. They welcomed children beyond those of the workers' families. In the early Victorian era, there was a substantial proportion of handicapped children, yet there were no facilities available for their education. The first school addressing this need emerged through the Glasgow Society for the Education of the Deaf and Dumb.[31] In Paisley, a school was established in 1823 by a group of gentlemen, providing elementary education and industrial training to six children by 1837.

4.3.5 Standard of Education in Subscription Schools

Many historians argue that the shortcomings of these subscription schools can be attributed to the ignorance and limited engagement of the subscribing parents and proprietors. Their primary concern often revolved around hiring the most economical teacher, and subscribers were frequently reluctant to intervene in the school's management. Furthermore, their interest was often short-lived. Despite these challenges, some subscription schools in Renfrewshire maintained a commendable standard of teaching and curriculum, earning government grants that reflected the educational standards of the time. By 1860 and 1861, 11 of these schools were receiving grants for certificated and pupil-teachers, with an additional two schools receiving grants for pupil-teachers. In 1864, 12 new schools were added to the list of those receiving annual grants. It's worth noting that some of them may have been eligible for grants for certificated teachers, as the grants were stated in one category. In total, 25 out of 53 schools in the region were benefiting from government grants.

The majority of subscription, works, industrial, and endowed schools in the first half of the century operated with the assistance of "monitors." The monitorial system was deemed essential due to the need for teachers to manage a significantly larger number of children, a scale beyond what is conceivable in modern Scotland. In 1866, the Argyle Commissioners noted that "a good master is quite able to interest and teach eighty or a hundred boys in the earlier years of the course."[32] The pioneer of such a system was Andrew Bell of Scotland and Joseph Lancaster, an English nonconformist.

Andrew Bell developed his "Madras system" while working at a male orphan asylum in Madras, India, during the late 18th century. In this system, children in each class were separated into teachers and pupils. The introduction of this system in Edinburgh occurred in 1810.[33]

J. Lancaster, on the contrary, appointed monitors in a school for underprivileged children. Typically, the monitors were older students, unlike the Madras system where bright boys assumed the role of teachers. These systems are primarily aimed at providing elementary instruction. In 1837, the monitorial system was implemented in all subscription schools in Renfrewshire, benefiting numerous underprivileged children with limited access to education. During the 1840s, these schools transitioned to a pupil-teacher system supported by the government. Among the 37 schools in 1837, six did not include arithmetic in their curriculum, mostly being industrial and a couple of factory schools. The standard curriculum in other schools comprised reading, writing, and arithmetic, with some incorporating grammar, geography, and bookkeeping. The John Neilston Institution was unique in offering secondary education alongside elementary education. These schools played a crucial role in educating underprivileged children on the essential skills of the time, with some emphasizing industrial training and basic reading. In 1837, most subscription schools held Sunday schools, providing an opportunity for full-time working children to receive some foundational education.

Due to the unavailability of information on 66 out of a total of 177 schools, and considering that some of them might be subscription schools, an approximate comparison is drawn regarding the growth in educational facilities offered by schools in this category. This analysis is presented in both Table XLIX and Table L, covering the period between 1837 and 1854-65. In Greenock and Eastwood, subscription schools catered to more children than any other type of school. In 1854, 42% of the students in Greenock were enrolled in these schools, whereas in Paisley, more children attended Church of Scotland and Adventure schools than subscription schools. By 1865, nearly 34% of children outside Paisley and Greenock, out of the total pupils in the county, were attending subscription schools—surpassing other types of schools.[34] However, in some areas, particularly rural parishes, there was a decline in the number of subscription schools, and scholars attending these schools decreased. In locations such as Inverkip and Inchinan, subscription schools were discontinued, and in Lockwinnock, one out of three schools had disappeared. This decline might be attributed to a decrease in population in these areas during this period, with respective drops of 43%, 3.6%, and 10%.[35] Conversely, in Abbey Paisley, despite a 26% fall in the number of pupils, the population increased by 15%. Limited sources indicate a decline in both the number of schools and scholars in this parish, prompting the parish minister in 1865 to express concerns about inadequate provisions to meet the educational demand. On the contrary, in Neilston, the number of subscription schools increased, but the number of scholars decreased to 23%. In this urban parish, where the population increased by 37%, it is suggested that children may have opted for adventure schools during this period.

Table XLIX:

Percentage of increase in the number of students in subscription schools in Renfrewshire between 1837, 1854, and 1865

	No. of scholars in subs. schools in 1837	No. of pupils in 1854	No. of pupils in 1865	% of increase
In the county (Outside Paisley and Greenock)	1,950	-	3,356	72
In Paisley and Greenock	966	1,968	-	104

Sources: PP/841 xix, PP 1854 lix, PP/867 xxvi.

The attendance percentage in subscription schools follows a parallel trend to other schools in the county, with 76% of pupils attending schools in 1865 outside Paisley and Greenock. The student enrollment in these schools was comparable to Stirlingshire but differed from the situation in Ayrshire, where twice as many scholars attended Church of Scotland schools as subscription schools. Consequently, the contribution of subscription schools to education was more significant in Renfrewshire than in Ayrshire, as indicated in Table L.

Table L:

Percentage of population and children attending subscription schools in Renfrewshire in 1837, 1854, and 1865

	1837		1854		1865		% increase in the population	% of the increase in pupils
	Population in areas where there was a subschool located	Children attending these schools	Population	Children	Population	Children		
In the country outside Paisley and Greenock	71,499	1,968	-	-	87,479	3,359	22	68
In Paisley and Greenock	59,031	966	69,339	1,968	-	-	17.5	106.0

Sources: *Census of Great Britain 1831 and 1851, Vol.II, Census of Scotland 1861 Vol, II, PP 184/xix, PP/854 lix and PP 1867 xxvi.*

Table LI:

Percentage of children in subscription schools out of the total children in Ayrshire, Renfrewshire, and Stirlingshire in 1854 and 1865

County	Year	Children attending subs. schools	Total pupils	%
Ayrshire	1865	5,858	31,739	18.5
Renfrewshire: 1. Paisley and Greenock	1854	1,968	8,401	23.4
2. Outside Paisley & Greenock	1865	3,356	10,019	33.3
Stirlingshire	1865	4,844	13,731	35.3

Sources: PP/867 xxvi.

4.4 Private Adventure Schools

4.4.1 Adventure Schools in Scotland and Renfrewshire

In the 19th century, urban areas in Scotland faced a shortage of schools, unable to meet the educational needs of all children. The population explosion in small cities strained the capacity of parish schools. [36] Additionally, in burghs, the existing burgh schools were inadequate to meet the demands of the upper and middle classes. Compounding the issue, many children in the burgeoning cities lived near the subsistence level, as their parents struggled to afford fees and couldn't spare the children from casual employment. The Education Act of 1845 assigned responsibility to parochial boards for the education of pauper children, but in the cities, the sheer number of such children made the task nearly impossible.

The Church of Scotland, Free Church, Catholic, and Episcopal churches, along with various other societies and individuals, endeavored to address the educational challenge. The fees in these church schools, excluding Catholic schools and certain rural parish schools, typically ranged from four to seven shillings per quarter for reading, writing, and arithmetic separately. Some subscription schools also maintained fee structures akin to these church schools. However, for the low-income group earning wages of 4–6 or 10–12 shillings a week, paying these fees for their children in the mid-19th century up to 1841 posed a significant challenge.[37] Consequently, there was ample opportunity for private enterprise in education, manifested in the form of adventure schools established by individuals for profit, featuring lower fees.

Many historians express a highly unfavorable opinion about these adventure schools. According to J. Scotland, these schools were often conducted in small single-room establishments where "a superannuated woman or a disabled man taught a few children" for a meager fee. J. Handly suggests that these schools were managed by cobblers, cripples, tailors, and others deemed unfit for any other occupation.[38] H.M. Inspectors also conveyed a very negative impression of these schools. One inspector, in 1841, described an adventure school where he observed 30 children, aged two through seven, crowded into a cellar measuring 10 feet square and 7 feet high, with a single window of 18 inches square that never opened. The children were huddled in a dark corner next to a bed with no light except from the fireplace, and there were no books available for reading.[39]

Some exceptions existed, such as the Edinburgh Institution in Edinburgh and the Gymnasium in Aberdeen. In 1867, there were 1,500 adventure schools in Scotland, with one third of them concentrated in the southwest around Glasgow. According to the inspectors' report, schools with fees of 6s a quarter were considered quite good, featuring average teachers and a reasonable curriculum, whereas those charging 2d a week were deemed valueless.[40] In the mid-19th century, Renfrewshire, particularly in larger towns like Paisley, Greenock, and Neilston, had a considerable number of adventure schools. The total count of adventure schools exceeded that of subscription and church schools in the county, with Paisley having a notably high number, constituting nearly half of the total schools in the burgh. In Greenock, where there was no parochial school, the education of children from the low-income group rested solely in the hands of private adventure schoolmasters, despite the relatively high fees. This suggests a genuine demand for education among such groups that other schools were not adequately addressing. Conversely, in Neilston, the number of adventure schools was limited. Among the larger and urban parishes like Eastwood and Paisley Abbey Parish, adventure schools were also scarce. In Eastwood, a higher number of subscription schools might have contributed to the smaller presence of adventure schools. Some of these schools were designated as academies, with a few having buildings erected through public subscription and then operated for profit. In a couple of instances, a schoolhouse or master's house was provided by a benevolent individual for the education of impoverished children, functioning for the mutual benefit of both the children and the master.[41]

4.4.2 Number of adventure schools and scholars in Renfrewshire

Based on the available data, albeit incomplete for 1837, it is evident that the number of adventure schools in Renfrewshire increased during the mid-19th century (Table LII). This surge was particularly notable in Paisley, where these schools received encouragement from the town council—a departure from previous centuries when the council had aimed to restrict adventure schools. The growing population and financial constraints faced by the council, exacerbated by a trade depression, necessitated alternative educational avenues. Despite the presence of various church schools, there remained a significant gap in educational provision. Unfortunately, concluding the number of scholars in these schools relative to the population increase is challenging due to some missing data as of 1837 (Table LIII).

Table LII:
No. of adventure schools in 1837, 1854, and 1865 in Renfrewshire

Name of the parish and burgh	1837		1854		1865	
	No. of adventure schools	Total Schools	No. of adventure schools	Total Schools	No. of adventure schools	Total Schools
Abbey Parish (Paisley)	4	17	-	-	1	15
Cathcart	1	3	-	-	1	3
Eaglesham	1	3	-	-	-	3
Eastwood	1	4	-	-	2	15

Name of the parish and burgh	1837		1854		1865	
	No. of adventure schools	Total Schools	No. of adventure schools	Total Schools	No. of adventure schools	Total Schools
Houston & Killellan	1	3	-	-	1	7
Kilbarchan	2	6	-	-	3	9
Kilmacolm	1	3	-	-	-	2
Lochwinnoch	1	6	-	-	1	6
Mearns	1	2	-	-	1	10
Neilston	1	7	-	-	7	17
Paisley	8	23	25	52	-	-
Greenock	7	14	11	29	-	-
Port Glasgow	1	3	-	-	1	10
Total	30	84	36	81	18	87

Sources: PP 1841 xix 653–83 and 261–65, PP 1854 lix, 512 and PP 1867:xxvi 212–17.

The growth of adventure schools and student enrollment varied across different regions of the county. In rural parishes like Eaglesham and Kilmacolm, a 13% decline in the number of scholars may be linked to a population decrease of 2% and 10%, respectively. In contrast, Abbey Paisley, encompassing both town and village, witnessed a 15% population increase but an 83% reduction in adventure school attendees, indicating insufficient attention to education in that parish. Subscription schools remained prominent in larger towns, but their role in educational provision was diminishing in other areas.

Table LIII:

Percentage of pupils in adventure schools in proportion to population in Paisley, Greenock, and Neilston in 1837, 1854, and 1865

Name of the parish/burgh	Paisley	Greenock	Neilston
Pop. in 1831	31,430	27,571	8,046
Pupil in 1851	621	409	43
Pop. in 1851	31,930	37,436	-
Pupil in 1854	2,085	932	-
Pop. in 1861	-	-	11,013
Pupil in 1865	-	-	240
% of increase in pop.	1.4	17.5	37.0
% of increase in pupil	236	128	458

Sources: *Census a/ Great Britain 1831 and/851 Vol. 11, Census of Scotland 1861, Vol. 11, PP 1841 xix, PP 1854 lix and PP 1867 xxiv.*

Typically, the curriculum in these adventure schools focused on reading and writing, with a few offering instruction in arithmetic, grammar, history, and geography. While some adventure schools in Paisley and Greenock garnered a positive reputation, certain teachers, like Mr. Peter Chalmers of Paisley, were particularly successful and remembered by the local community. Except for some schools in Greenock, the fees in most adventure schools were very affordable. In 1865, many adventure schools were modest in size and poorly situated.

Despite having substantial school buildings, often containing four or five classrooms, none of them received government grants. In a few instances, such as in Cathcart and Eastwood, as well as some in Paisley and Greenock, the schoolhouses were relatively large. In certain schools in Paisley, Greenock, and Cathcart, the student population exceeded a hundred, but in others, the number was as low as 50, and in a few cases, attendance was as minimal as 15. It was the norm for adventure schools, except for those in Greenock, Paisley, and Cathcart, to be overseen by a single teacher, reflecting the common practice of the time. Notably, none of the teachers in these Renfrewshire adventure schools held teaching certifications.

Despite the poor condition of the schoolhouse and noncertificated teachers, these adventure schools were widely attended in the county. Probably the reason was that the parents wanted their children to learn something quickly and leave school for work. The Commissioners made this point about a reading test made at a mill in Ayrshire. Asking why the parents sent the children to the ill-ventilated adventure schools, ill-provided with desks and maps in preference to parochial and Free Church schools, they concluded "Because the master of the adventure schools manages to prepare the children to pass the reading test sooner than other teachers who have to educate them to pass the standard of the revised code."[43] Moreover, in these schools the fees were also lower (2–3d a week).

When assessing the proportion of students attending adventure schools in Ayrshire, Renfrewshire, and Stirlingshire, it becomes evident that these schools made a more substantial contribution to Renfrewshire and a comparatively lesser impact in Ayrshire (Table LIV).

Table LIV:
Percentage of scholars in adventure schools in proportion to total pupils in Ayrshire, Renfrewshire, and Stirlingshire

County	Year	No. of adventure school	Total scholars	%
Ayrshire	1865	2,785	31,739	9
Renfrewshire: 1. Paisley and Greenock	1854	3,017	8,401	35.9
2. Outside Paisley and Greenock	1865	676	10,019	6.7
Stirlingshire	1865	2,352	13,131	17

Source: PP 1867 xxvi, 37–50, 212–24.

4.5 Conclusion

Secular entities played a significant role in educating children in Renfrewshire. The state collaborated with various religious and non-religious organizations to facilitate the establishment of educational institutions. Legislative measures and financial support were provided to maintain specific educational standards, primarily focusing on foundational learning before children entered the workforce. With inspections conducted to determine eligibility for grants, approximately 64 schools in Renfrewshire likely met the required standards. The presence of certified teachers increased, and schools underwent annual inspections, with their reputation hinging on the inspectors' reports. While this ensured a maintained standard, there was a downside as the pursuit of maximum grants often led to a narrowed curriculum, emphasizing essential subjects such as reading, writing, and arithmetic.

The town councils in the burghs conscientiously fulfilled their responsibilities in educating middle-class children and, to some extent, those from lower-income families. Despite the commendable efforts of churches and town councils, a substantial number of children would have lacked access to education if not for the various subscription and adventure schools. These schools, with a few exceptions, primarily served the needs of underprivileged children. Industrial schools provided practical training for boys and girls, often incorporating basic reading skills, while some also included instruction in writing and arithmetic. Factory schools offered working children an opportunity for literacy through half-time or night classes. In several instances, philanthropists' donations led to the establishment of schools, particularly in prominent towns like Paisley and Greenock, helping alleviate the strain on educational resources. The recognition of educational challenges arising from urbanization and population growth was evident in the community's response.

Divergent opinions exist regarding the educational effectiveness of adventure schools; however, their role in preventing a substantial number of children from facing illiteracy is apparent. Adventure schools played a crucial role, especially in significant urban centers like Paisley and Neilston, where affordable subscription schools were lacking. In contrast, in larger town parishes such as Greenock, Eastwood, and Abbey Paisley, subscription schools took precedence over adventure schools. Notably, in Greenock, certain adventure schools levied fees comparable to those in church schools, potentially attracting more students due to lower costs. Furthermore, many subscription and adventure schools conducted

Sunday schools, aiding literacy for children engaged in full-time work.

Between 1837 and 1865, subscription and adventure schools in the burghs witnessed a rise in the number of students, as indicated by the available albeit incomplete data. Instances reveal that in certain locations, the count of subscription and adventure schools dwindled, either due to a decline in population or the neglect of educational facilities. In 1854, the attendance percentages at subscription schools were 42% in Greenock, 12% in Paisley, 31% in Abbey Paisley in 1861, and 34% in the county beyond these three places in 1865. Adventure schools accounted for 41% of students in Paisley and 29% in Greenock in 1854. By 1865, 7.40% of the total scholars in the county were enrolled in adventure schools.44

From the comprehensive analysis provided in these chapters, a tentative conclusion can be drawn that there was a general uptick in the enrollment of children across various school types, with a few exceptions. Notably, the Paisley Abbey area stands out as an anomaly. In most other regions, there was a heightened awareness of the educational requirements for children. However, it remains evident that a significant number of children were still not enrolled in any school during the 1860s and 1870s.45 This underscores the necessity for increased state intervention in education.

Chapter 5: Quality of Educational Facilities

5.1 Qualification of Teachers in Different Schools

The adequacy of educational facilities within a school hinges on the quality of teaching, which is directly correlated with the qualifications of the educators. Before the mid-19th century, formal training for parish teachers was scarce in Scotland, as dedicated training institutions did not emerge until the 1830s. In 1845, Mr. Gordon, H.M. Inspector, conducted a survey of schools in Clackmannan, Linlithgow, and Renfrew, revealing that only 36 out of 166 teachers had undergone formal training, with 13 of them studying for a brief period of two months at normal schools.[1] Subsequently, as the government began promoting training and certification through grants, more parish teachers started enrolling in training schools. This initiative led to an increase in certified teachers within the Church of Scotland, Free Church, and subscription schools.

Before delving into discussions about the qualifications of teachers, it is essential to elucidate the meaning of certification and the methods employed for teacher training. Certification denotes a qualification obtained from various training establishments. The inaugural training college, the Dundee Vale Seminary, was established in 1836 by the Glasgow Educational Society. Dr. Rusk emphasizes that "it was to a private

Educational Society, and not to the Church, that Scotland was indebted for the first Training College."² The E.C.C. took control of it in 1841, offering a nine-month course. Following the Disruption in 1845, David Stow and the entire staff departed, leading to the opening of the Free Church normal school in 1846. The course duration expanded to 12 months in 1848 and further extended to two years in 1851. Sessions ran from January to December, with a nine-week vacation in July and August.

In the normal schools of the Church of Scotland located in Edinburgh and Glasgow, both genders participated in practical teaching lessons for one hour daily within the practicing schools. The female curriculum emphasized needlework and domestic economy, replacing subjects like physical science, Latin, and advanced mathematics. The prescribed textbooks for theoretical education in the training colleges of both the Church of Scotland and the Free Church included D. Stow's "Training System," Morrison's "Manual," and Locke's "Thoughts on Education." The program culminated in a government examination for a certificate of merit, organized in classes after a two-year duration in the Free Church seminary and after 12 months in the Church of Scotland's normal school.³

Dr. Fearon, representing the Schools Enquiry Commission during his visit to Scotland, asserted that there was a consistent influx of competent teachers from the universities into Scottish secondary schools. Nevertheless, opinions diverged on the significance of university degrees. In his 1868 autobiography, Rev. J. Hamilton Gray expressed his perspective: "Glasgow College was a commendable institution for acquiring general information and accumulating knowledge on diverse subjects, but it fell short in instilling profound scholarship."4

Glasgow, Edinburgh, Aberdeen, and St. Andrews universities featured a curriculum in Arts that encompassed Latin, Greek, Logic, mathematics, moral, and natural philosophy. The 1858 Act introduced English Literature and established honors examinations in Classics, mathematics, and physical science, although these were infrequently pursued. Graduation gained popularity, and by 1837, the duration of university courses extended to over four years.

The university curriculum encompassed natural and civil history, incorporating poetry, versification, geography, discoveries, chronology, the British Constitution, as well as the histories of Egypt, Greece, and Rome. Additionally, the curriculum covered subjects such as chemistry, mineralogy, geology, meteorology, botany, zoology, anatomy, and animal and vegetable physiology.5

The examination for the A.M. degree (equivalent to the M.A. degree) was thorough and extended over seven days. At Edinburgh University, women could obtain a certificate in Arts by passing any three of the following subjects through local examinations: literature, Latin, Greek, logic, moral philosophy, political economy, mathematics, experimental physics, botany, and zoology. It can be asserted that individuals who underwent studies in these universities were academically well-qualified to teach at both secondary and elementary schools.

Information on the quality of teaching is derived from government grants allocated to various schools for certified teachers. The Reports of the H.M. Assistant Commission provide insights into the qualifications of burgh schoolmasters. In Renfrewshire, around 1860, there were approximately 48 certified teachers. Notably, some schools received a relatively high grant for certified teachers, possibly indicating the presence of two to three such teachers. For instance, the John Neilson Institution of Paisley received a £91 grant for certified teachers in 1861, boasting six certified teachers in the 1870s. Certain schools were also granted amounts ranging from £30 to £45 in this regard. Considering that grants to other schools in this category ranged from £20 to £25, it can be inferred that schools receiving more than £25 might have had more than one certified teacher. Additionally, the actual number of certified teachers could be higher than indicated, as some burgh schools employed certified masters without receiving grants, and these were not reflected in the returns. Therefore, it is conceivable that there were around 55 to 60 such teachers in the county during the 1860s, among a total of 248 masters and mistresses.[7]

Before the implementation of grants for certified teachers, the qualifications of parish teachers held significant importance. The position of a parish teacher was appealing; while the salary may not have been substantial, it exceeded that of almost all other schools in the parish. The transition from assembly to parish schools was considered a form of "promotion."[8] Individuals with some educational background were inclined to join these schools, viewing them as a stepping stone to more desirable employment, particularly within the church. The NSA provided information on certain clerical masters in the parish of Erskine in Renfrewshire, mirroring a trend observed in several parishes across different counties, where previous masters were engaged in ecclesiastical roles in the 1830s. In 1837, within the county, numerous parish schools had masters who had attended

Glasgow University, with five having completed the course. In Scotland in 1827, with a total of 906 parish schools, over 400 had masters who had undergone a four-year university course, leaving only 250 schools where the dominie had no college education.[9]

The oversight of the appointment of parish teachers by the presbyteries remained stringent until 1861. Prospective candidates were required to submit to the presbytery a record of their selection by the ministers, a copy of their oath before the justice of the peace, a testimonial affirming their character, and evidence verifying their qualifications.

The parish master underwent examination by a committee of the presbytery and was appointed by the heritors. The masters could face removal if found lacking in knowledge of any subject they were required to teach after their selection. Since the late 18th century, numerous vacancies were advertised in the press, resulting in a competitive selection process. With the introduction of the teachers' training system and the support of government grants, many parish dominies pursued certification. In 1861, nine parish schools in Renfrewshire had masters who were certificated. By 1865, two additional schools received annual grants, indicating a likelihood that they had acquired certificated teachers by that time.

In Free Church schools, masters were elected by church bodies, with the Deacons' Court initiating the appointment and the Free Church Presbytery confirming it. Subsequently, teachers were required "to be introduced to his charge by the office bearers of the congregation, the Deacons' Court being thereafter responsible for the day-to-day running of the school."[10] Similar to parish teachers, they underwent thorough examinations before the appointment. Following the Disruption, numerous accomplished teachers from parish schools joined the Free Church and took up positions in its schools. The church also established its training schools, increasing the number of certificated teachers in its schools. When school boards assumed control, Free Church schools exhibited a notably higher proportion of certificated teachers compared to those of the Established Church. By 1860, nine Free Church institutions in Renfrewshire employed certificated teachers.

When the school boards assumed control, Free Church schools exhibited a significantly higher percentage of certificated teachers compared to those in the Established Church.[11] In Renfrewshire by 1860, nine Free Church institutions had employed certificated teachers.

The consensus among scholars is that Catholic schools across Scotland faced a shortage of proficient teachers. The salaries offered, particularly for certificated teachers, were not enticing, primarily relying on fees. These fees were not substantial, given that the scholars were predominantly impoverished Irish, particularly in the west of Scotland. Additionally, there was a deficiency in training facilities for Catholic teachers in Scotland. While Free Church training colleges did not impose denominational restrictions on students, it wasn't until 1872 that a Catholic individual enrolled in these colleges. Most Catholic teachers sought training in schools in Ireland, resulting in a persistently low number of trained teachers until the close of the 19th century. In Renfrewshire in 1860, only one Catholic school received a grant for certificated teachers. In other schools, the primary qualification for teachers was the ability to instruct in reading, writing, and basic arithmetic. While deemed sufficient for that era, such schools were deemed less efficient compared to parish and Free Church schools.

Burgh schoolmasters enjoyed higher salaries compared to parish dominies, with substantial competition for positions such as rector and masters of different departments. The examinations for these roles were more rigorous than those for parish schools, typically covering English, arithmetic, Bible studies, British history, bookkeeping, navigation, Latin, and Greek.[13] Most teachers in larger schools were usually graduates of a Scottish university, while those in smaller institutions needed to have attended a university or obtained training and certification after the 1840s. Many Burgh schoolmasters were recognized for their scholarly achievements and success. Several served in their roles for 20–30 years, exemplified by James Peddle of the English School in Paisley, who dedicated half a century to the cause of education for the children of the burgh.

In subscription schools, aspiring teachers needed to gain approval from the committee of subscribers, with the concurrence of the parish minister. In factory schools, selection was conducted by employers, proprietors, or subscribing laborers, who could hold the office at their discretion since they contributed to the school's construction. In many instances, teachers for such schools were required to possess the ability to teach reading, writing, and arithmetic. Nevertheless, by 1865, numerous subscription schools in Renfrewshire had appointed certificated teachers. Adventure schools, where the master was self-employed, did not place a strong emphasis on specific qualifications.

5.2 Pupil-Teacher Ratio

An indicator of the quality of teaching facilities is the pupil-teacher ratio, and the prevailing ratios in different types of schools are analyzed. In the 19th century, it was common, except in burgh schools, to instruct a considerable number of students from various age groups in a single room. A typical scenario involved managing 100–150 children aged 5 to 13, with the responsibility of teaching them three to six subjects at different levels. Professor Laurie's estimation suggested that a parish teacher had to conduct a minimum of 25 separate lessons daily. This led to the division of classes into groups, utilizing monitors before the 1840s and later employing pupil-teachers. In 1837, monitors assisted masters in teaching a large number of children in all parochial schools and 56 other schools. The pupil-teacher system, introduced by Kay-Shuttleworth's minute on August 25, 1846, and supported by government grants, replaced the monitorial system. By the 1860s in Renfrewshire, 48 to 55 schools received grants for pupil-teachers. Larger schools often employed three to four pupil-teachers.[14]

A table has been compiled to illustrate the pupil-teacher ratio in various school types in 1837, 1854, and 1865. When pupil-teachers and assistant teachers were factored in, the ratio was lower. In burgh schools, the assistant teachers, who were certificated and had separate classes, were considered in the ratio (see Table LV).

Table LV:
Pupil-teacher ratio in different types of schools in Renfrewshire in 1837, 1854, and 1865

Type of school	No. of schools	No. of teachers	No. Of scholars	Pupil-teacher ratio	No. of schools	No. of teachers	No. of scholars	Pupil-teacher ratio
Parochial	13	13	904	69.53	13	16+5 PT + 3 asst.	1,742[(1)]	108.87 / 68.41
Church of Scotland	7	8	584	73.0	32	38	3,282[(2)]	86.36
Free Church	-	-	-	-	15	23	1,772	77.04
Catholic	3	3	260	86.66	13	13	1,452	111.61
Episcopal	1	1	72	72.0	5[(3)]	5	327	65.4
Side school	-	-	-	-	4	4+3PT	424	106.0
Burgh school	6	10	829	82.9	5	25	1,670[(1)]	66.8
Sub.	37	40	2,916	72.9	53	74+6PT	5,324	72.95 / 66.55
P. Adventure	30	32	1,812	65.1	54	72	3,693[(1)]	51.29

(1)   Including the pupil-teachers.

(2)   There might be some mistake as in Paisley the school under Church of Scotland might include the burgh schools in PP 1854 lix–512.

(3)   There is also a gap as in Greenock, the number of teachers mentioned in three Episcopal schools was two in the same return.

Sources: PP 1841 xix 653–83, 261–69, PP /854 /ix 5/2, PP 1967 xxvi 212–17, PP /86718 xxix I /9–75.

Private adventure schools had a lower number of children per teacher, primarily because these schools were typically small, with 14–15 pupils and rarely exceeding 50. In Paisley, Greenock, and Cathcart, some adventure schools were larger with more than one teacher. However, the size of these schools did not necessarily correlate with their overall quality compared to a parish, Free Church, and certain subscription schools where the pupil-teacher ratio was higher. Most of these latter schools were overseen by certificated teachers, while none of the adventure schools could claim such certification. Schools with a higher pupil-teacher ratio and under-trained teachers generally demonstrated better management than those with a lower number of scholars under untrained teachers. The ratio was also elevated in Catholic schools in towns, reflecting the insufficient number of schools to meet the educational demand of the expanding Catholic population. Additionally, the Catholics, being economically disadvantaged, could not afford more than one teacher in their schools.

A distinction in ratios existed between urban and rural areas, with the ratio typically being lower in rural regions. In urban areas, especially due to rapid population growth, schools were often crowded, except for adventure schools. Interestingly, in certain rural areas like Eaglesham, the ratio resembled that of urban areas. Adventure schools, Free Church establishments, female industrial schools, and parish schools were generally not overcrowded. Nevertheless, it's important to note that the pupil-teacher ratio alone does not serve as a fully satisfactory indicator of the quality of educational facilities during that era. While the situation in Stirlingshire was nearly identical, the ratio was higher in Ayrshire (see Table LVI).

Table LVI:
Pupil-teacher ratio in Ayrshire, Renfrewshire, and Stirlingshire in 1854 and 1865

County	Year	No. of scholars	No. of teachers	Ratio
Ayrshire	1865	31,739	306	103.73
Renfrewshire: 1. Paisley and Greenock	1854	8,401	125	67.2
2. Outside Paisley and Greenock*	1865	9,403	116	81.1
Stirlingshire	1865	13,731	187	73.0

*Incomplete data for Abbey Paisley Sources: PP 1867 xxvi 37–50, 212–24.

5.3 Curriculum

Information about the curriculum in various schools is available for 1837 and for burgh schools in 1867. Examining the curriculum generally followed in 19th-century Scotland and that of Renfrewshire in 1837 provides insight into the subjects taught in schools throughout the county. Typically, parish and various church schools focused on instruction in the fundamental three Rs (reading, writing, arithmetic) and religion, with only two to four exceptions. Most of these schools also included grammar, mathematics, history, and geography in their curriculum. Additionally, subjects like Latin, Greek, French, and drawing were taught, varying from parish to parish based on the teacher's proficiency and the preferences of the heritors.

In 1837, arithmetic was not part of the curriculum in 14 adventure schools and six subscription schools. The subscription schools, primarily industrial, aimed to provide professional training to scholars, focusing on reading and writing. In one female industrial school, even reading was not included. Other subscription and adventure schools primarily emphasized reading, writing, and arithmetic, while a few subscription schools also included religion, geography, history, and mathematics in their teachings. Burgh schools, in addition to the basic subjects, featured Latin, Greek, English, mathematics, history, geography, and drawing in their curriculum.

Religious instruction was "the center of our educational system in Scotland... by a public opinion as strong as law."[16] According to Dr. Gordon, religious teaching typically involved narratives from the Bible accompanied by historical explanations rather than rigid dogma. The Argyle Commissioners noted that the shorter catechism was deemed unsuitable for many children. Consequently, the significance of both the Bible and catechism was not uniformly apparent. Typically, the mother's catechism was intended for younger children, while older children studied the shorter catechism.

English studies typically included a widespread emphasis on reading and spelling. Occasionally, teachers would dictate a passage from a book, and students were required to memorize it for the subsequent day's lesson. Some schools also incorporated the teaching of grammar. In arithmetic, a primary focus was on counting, with an emphasis on memorizing tables. Writing, the final component of the three Rs, encompassed the practice of English alphabets, words, and numbers.

Instruction in German, French, Latin, and Greek encompassed reading, writing, spelling, and occasionally grammar. However, the number of students studying classical languages experienced a decline in the mid-19th century, even within burgh schools. Dr. Wilson attributed this decline to a decrease in the teaching proficiency of educators between 1850 and 1865. In parish schools, fewer than one percent of students opted for Latin, and only one in 200 showed a preference for Greek, both of which had a quarterly cost of five to six shillings.[17] The number of children studying French increased, with fees exceeding seven shillings. However, very few schools offered instruction in German, and none in Renfrewshire provided such lessons.

Mathematics studies comprised Euclid, trigonometry, navigation, mensuration, land measurement, geometry, and occasionally a basic introduction to algebra. According to N.S.A. reports, approximately five to six percent of children in parish schools engaged in such advanced lessons. In other schools, very few students attended these more specialized classes. History lessons generally focused on significant events in England and Scotland, providing a "general sequence of the landmarks of history." Geography was often treated as a catalog subject. Drawing primarily involved "freehand sketching from flat examples."[18] In industrial schools for girls, instruction in needlework was provided. Boys in industrial schools received technical training, including activities like tailoring, shoemaking, and practical teaching in agriculture.

Table LVII:
No. of schools in which different subjects were followed in 1837 in Ayrshire, Renfrewshire, and Stirlingshire.

Subjects	Ayrshire(1)		Renfrewshire (1)		Stirlingshire (l)	
	Non- paro	Paro (2)	Non- paro	Paro (2)	Non- paro	Paro (2)
English	154	39	92	18	93	29
Gaelic	-	-	-	-	-	-
Greek	20	23	9	7	4	15
Latin	45	35	21	10	16	23
Modern languages	9	19	6	6	10	11
Mathematics	49	29	23	8	22	22
Arithmetic	134	38	72	15	71	27
Geography	84	36	43	13	47	28
History	85	25	30	11	35	21
Religious instruction	rs1	39	89	18	91	29
Singing	17	7	27	5	19	9
Drawing	14	2	12	4	8	6
Instruction is given in gardening, agriculture and mechanical	-	-	1	1	-	-
Total	155	56(2)	93	18(2)	96	40(2)

(1) 211 schools out of 255 answers to the queries of C.C. Min Ayrshire. In Renfrewshire, the number was 111 out of 177 and in Stirlingshire, it was 136 out of 167 schools.
(2) These parochial schools included 12 other schools in Ayrshire, 3 in Renfrewshire, and 17 in Stirlingshire.
Source: PP 1841 xix, 782.

The percentage of schools covering the fundamental subjects was nearly identical in these counties, indicating that Renfrewshire's curriculum was also representative of other industrial counties.

5.4 Discipline and School Life

In the 19th century, teachers typically had to manage a large number of children from various age groups within a single class, presenting challenges in maintaining discipline. To address this issue, a monitorial system was implemented in the early part of the century, followed by the pupil-teacher system after the 1840s. Corporal punishment was widespread, with canes, rulers, and umbrella ribs used as alternatives to the tawse. Typically, children were disciplined by being beaten on the palm. In extreme cases, unruly children might be confined to the coal bunker, or teachers resorted to piercing a pupil's ear with sharp-pointed pens. Horace Mann remarked that "the highest tension of authority which I anywhere witnessed was in the Scottish schools." He acknowledged a bond of attachment between teacher and pupil, stemming not only from affection but also from a sense of awe.[19]

Records indicate that in 1837, in Renfrewshire, corporal punishment was administered in all parish schools and 58 other schools. Some schools opted for the punishment of demoting a student's place in the class. Another practice involved students standing on their seats throughout the lesson. Occasionally, additional tasks were assigned as a form of punishment. For irregular attendance and disruptive behavior, children were sometimes isolated from others until deemed fit to rejoin the class. In extreme cases, a pupil in one school was placed in a pitch-black hole.[20] As an alternative to punishment, a method employed was to motivate children through prizes for exemplary behavior. The prize system was widely adopted in both parish and burgh schools. Many subscription and adventure schools also utilized a prize award system. It was not uncommon for a local landowner to contribute prizes to the parish schools, and subscribers might collectively contribute to purchasing prizes for subscription schools. Some burgh schools saw the presentation of medals or prizes by local philanthropists. In most instances, it was the responsibility of the teacher to provide the prize, with the award often signifying promotion to a higher class.

In both Scotland and Renfrewshire, books were typically awarded as prizes. In 1837, rewards of some kind were provided in all parish schools and 65 other schools. Burgh schools held their prize-giving ceremony annually in July following the annual examination. For instance, in Greenock, the Campbell Prize included a box of mathematical instruments. Notably, Horace Mann observed that among European countries, competition and emulation were particularly strong in Scotland and France.[21] Discipline was upheld through a combination of punishment and the bestowal of prizes. Rewards served to motivate children toward achieving positive results and exhibiting appropriate behavior.

The school year was structured into quarters, with a harvest vacation lasting four to six weeks and a winter holiday spanning 10–12 days. Some schools lacked a standardized vacation system, and breaks were granted based on the preferences of the teacher or subscribers. During the summer, school hours typically ran from 9 or 9:30 a.m. to 4 p.m., with a one-hour break. In winter, the schedule shifted from 10 in the morning to three in the afternoon, with a half-hour break.

5.5 The Quality of School Buildings

Until 1873, there is no comprehensive classification of the conditions of all school buildings available. However, insights can be gleaned from various parliamentary papers and the N.S.A. regarding the state of school housing in Renfrewshire. Many of the 103 schools in the 1867 report were described as either in disrepair or overcrowded, while some were noted as excellent. The Burgh Council records documented repeated requests for repair works, with frequent complaints about inadequate buildings and locations. This was a prevalent issue in Scotland during the mid-19th century and not a unique characteristic of Renfrewshire. In 1867, the commissioners criticized the education system, stating, "At present there is no authority to initiate, to administer, or to superintend. Schools sprang up where they are not required, and buildings may be good or unsuitable."[22]

The NSA revealed that some schools in Renfrewshire were in poor condition. The English school in Paisley had to be relocated in the early part of the century. James Peddle, the schoolmaster, wrote a letter to the council, providing insight into the nature of the buildings at that time. He expressed,

> This schoolroom [is] far too small for the accommodation of the number of scholars that attended. Indeed, a change of place would, on many accounts, be extremely desirable. The situation, more open or at a distance from a confined, nasty, vicious neighborhood... would certainly be favorable to the health, moral, and general improvement of the youth.[23]

Mr. Peter Fraser of Greenock rejected the appointment to the commercial school in 1855 due to its unfavorable location and inadequate classrooms. Consequently, the school remained vacant and was eventually sold in 1863. In 1867, the Port Glasgow Burgh School building was in poor condition, and the school's location was deemed unsatisfactory. The building had a low roof, and its original use was dual-purpose, with the upper part serving as a courthouse and the lower level as a school. In Renfrew, the Grammar school was initially held in the session house in the early 19th century.[24]

In Johnstone of Abbey Paisley, all schools except the ragged school were in poor condition. It is noted that:

> the police burgh of Johnstone, with a population within the burghal boundaries of upwards of 7,000, is entirely lacking in the means of efficient education for the inhabitants. This need had long been felt, and various efforts had been made over time to improve the state of affairs. However, sectarianism had bitterly caused the frustration of all such attempts.

Both the Free and Established Church ministers affirmed that "there is no schoolroom in the burgh of Johnstone that is even decent, and no teachers of any standing except in the ragged school and its master."[25] The Catholic school was located in the upper story of an old cotton mill. The school on Church Street was described as being held in a very small room, and the overcrowded premises were not kept clean and tidy. Many parents in Johnstone, who could afford to do so, opted to send their children to school in Paisley. However, for others, the only alternative was the side school in Quarrellton village. In Kilmacolm parish, the side school was situated in a thatched house with one schoolroom and one room for the teacher. Factory schools in Eaglesham had poorly constructed floors. The majority of adventure school buildings were in unsuitable conditions—small and overcrowded. The parish schools of Kilmacolm, Kilbarchan, and Neilston had to be relocated or repaired periodically due to poor conditions or unfavorable locations.

It would be an exaggeration to assert that all schools in the county were in such poor condition. Several school buildings were indeed excellent. Two of the Free Church schools were reported to have good accommodation, and others met government standards, with 11 of them receiving building grants. Some of the works schools offered superior accommodation, such as the Busby Works School in Mearns, which had four well-heated and ventilated rooms. The female industrial school room at Eaglesham was also of good quality. The ragged school in Johnstone was described as an excellent one-story building erected in accordance with government plans. Additionally, the Howwood school in the village of Lochwinnoch parish, easily transferred to the school board in 1873, was noteworthy. The adventure school in Cathcart and Eastwood had four to five rooms. In Port Glasgow, six out of seven schools were reported to provide good accommodation. The John Neilson Institution in Paisley comprised four spacious rooms with accommodation for 600–700 students, featuring a room measuring 67 ft by 33 ft and another measuring 62 ft by 33 ft, with a ceiling height of 23 ft 11 in.[26]

The parish schoolhouses in Eaglesham and Kilmacolm were outstanding. Eastwood and Neilston parish schools had three classrooms each, while Kilbarchan, Inverkip, Lochwinnoch, and

Cathcart schools each had one schoolroom and one classroom. Furthermore, 11 of these schools were receiving building grants, indicating that they were in relatively good condition. In 1837, eight parochial and 28 other schools had playgrounds attached to them, and the parish schools were situated in positions conducive to playing, with every convenience provided.[27]

In the burghs during the early 19th century, several schools had to be relocated due to poor building conditions or unfavorable locations. However, by the 1850s, most of them were reported to be in good condition, except for Port Glasgow School. Renfrew's Blysthwood testimonial was well-suited for educating children, featuring a good playground with a covered shed for inclement weather. The Paisley Academy had a well-provided building with six classrooms and space for 580 scholars. Similarly, the Greenock Academy had numerous rooms, including one exclusively for advanced girls in the upper classes, along with separate playgrounds for boys and girls. The building underwent generous repairs by the directors, providing accommodation for 1,086 scholars, indicating its substantial size.[28]

In 1865, 15 schoolhouses in Renfrewshire were classified as "excellent, good, spacious," featuring "first-class school rooms" or "newly built according to government plans." Another 24 schools had one or two "classrooms" and one "school room," while two additional schools had three to four rooms, quality not specified. The remaining 41 schools out of 103 were single-room schools, some in poor repair and bad condition. A similar situation was observed in Ayrshire during the same year, where 118 out of 252 schoolhouses were reported as good, spacious, or excellent. While some consisted of a single room, they were spacious enough to accommodate a large number of children.

Most parish schools were in good condition, and several sessional, Free, and Catholic church schools were described as new stone buildings with slate roofs. However, others were old and in disrepair, with a few lacking sufficient desks and furniture,[29] indicating a comparable condition.

5.6 Availability of Equipment in the Schools

In the 19th century, even parish schools were inadequately equipped. The commissioners noted in 1867, "the school apparently may be adequate, or there may not be a bench to write at or a blackboard or map throughout the length and breadth of the whole district." Even in parish schools, a complete set of apparatus was rarely available. Children often had to sit at double desks facing each other, and there was a shortage of maps and globes in some schools, with certain institutions lacking even a blackboard.[30]

There is limited data available on the equipment in Renfrewshire schools. However, based on the grants awarded and the subjects taught, some understanding can be derived. Between 1833 and 1855, Established Church schools received a grant of £32-5-2.3/4d. specifically for books and maps. During the same period, the Free Church's allocation for books and maps was £14-9. The Episcopal and Catholic church received building grants, but no specific grant was designated for books and maps.[31] Practical instruction in tailoring and shoemaking, requiring specific tools, was provided in industrial and reformatory schools. The Pollock Industrial School, for instance, received £133 as an industrial grant. In Paisley, the Ragged and Reformatory School had a workshop, and some agricultural instruction took place in the field. Alongside industrial equipment, the annual grant from the C.C.E. could encompass funds for maps, desks, books, and other necessities. In 1864, approximately 40 schools in the county, excluding Paisley and Greenock, received annual grants.[32]

Burgh and Grammar schools offered various subjects that required specific equipment, particularly for practical applications like geography, geometry, land surveying, navigation, and more. The Greenock Town Council documented a payment of £78 to Mr. L. Lamont, the schoolmaster in 1800, for "different instruments purchased by him for the use of the school," likely for the Grammar school.[33] Furthermore, since there were no complaints about the lack of instruction in these schools from the commissioners in 1867, it can be asserted that these institutions were adequately equipped with sufficient desks, maps, books, and other necessary materials.

5.7 Conclusion

The quality of teaching in a school depends on the qualifications of the teachers. Before the mid-19th century, there was a shortage of formal training for parish teachers in Scotland. Training institutions for teachers started appearing in the 1830s. A survey conducted in 1845 showed that only a few teachers had received formal training. However, more teachers started enrolling in training schools when the government began promoting training and certification through grants. As a result, the number of certified teachers in different schools increased.

Certification is a qualification obtained from training establishments. The first training college, Dundee Vale Seminary, was established in 1836. After that, training schools expanded and increased the duration of courses. Academic training included practical teaching lessons in Edinburgh and Glasgow. Female students focused on needlework and domestic skills. The training program concluded with a government examination for a certificate of merit.

Competent teachers also came from universities, although there are differing opinions on the importance of university degrees. University arts programs covered subjects like Latin, Greek, mathematics, philosophy, and literature. The curriculum also included various scientific disciplines.

Government grants allocated to schools provided information about the quality of teaching. Reports revealed the qualifications of schoolmasters. Some schools received higher grants, indicating the presence of certified teachers. However, there might have been more certified teachers who still needed to be reflected in the records. Some schools were in poor condition and needed to be relocated or repaired.

While some schools were in poor condition, others had excellent facilities. School buildings varied in size and quality. Parochial and other schools had playgrounds attached to them. Burgh schools gradually improved their conditions and were reportedly in good shape. Even parish schools needed more proper equipment in the 19th century. Some schools needed better equipment, including furniture, desks, maps, and blackboards. Grants were given for books, maps, and equipment in different schools. Industrial and reformatory schools provided practical instruction with specific tools.

Chapter 6: Regional Variations in Attendance

6.1 Introduction

The mid-19th-century attendance of students in Renfrewshire schools exhibited variations across villages and towns. These differences can be ascribed to diverse economic factors such as poverty, child labor, immigrant communities, and population distribution. However, a comprehensive analysis of these variables hinges on the availability of primary data and information for the study period. Utilizing data from the 1871 census and other parliamentary papers can offer pertinent insights into the number of children (aged 5–13) receiving education relative to the total population in villages and towns. Information about the overall number of unenrolled children is accessible for the entire county, as well as specifically for Paisley and Greenock during the same period. Additionally, evidence regarding the attendance of scholars out of the total enrolled is obtainable for the entire county in 1865, excluding Paisley and Greenock towns and a section of Abbey Paisley.

6.2 Child Labor

In the 1840s, Factory Legislation was enacted to restrict the employment of children under 13 years old, mandating at least 30 days of attendance every six months for those in this age group.

Before this legislation, there was widespread employment of children. In the 19th century, child wage labor was limited due to abundant adolescent labor in most towns. Girls typically did not enter domestic service before the age of 13. Nevertheless, in textile areas or towns, opportunities for wage labor existed for children under 13 or 14. In silk and cotton spinning mills, children aged 9–13 worked for nine hours a day or 48 hours a week. However, the number of children under 13 years employed in textile mills remained relatively low. The Factory Inspector's Report (F.I.R.) of 1839 indicated that less than 1% of workers in Paisley cotton mills and 5% in silk mills were under 13 years old.[1] The data depicting the number of children engaged in various occupations in Paisley during the 1850s is presented in Table LVIII.

Table LVIII:

Employment distribution of the 10-14 age group by sex. Paisley, % weighted samples 1851 (all children)

	Boys	Girls
Textile (non-weaving)	38	35
Textile (hand-weaving)	2	1
Other occupations	7	7
Not employed	16	26
At school	38	30
(100%)	389	495

Source: Table 7.5, Brenda E.A. Collins, op. cit., 145.

As a result, 40% of children aged 10–14 engaged in labor were employed in non-weaving textile mills. Legal regulations did not constrain employment in bleachfields, handloom weaving factories, and domestic workshops until the 1860s. Children were involved in various tasks in print works, bleachfields, shawl warehouses, and supported weavers, often without due consideration for working hours, working conditions, and the age at which labor commenced.[2] Children as young as 11 or 12 were engaged in tasks related to textile production, particularly in roles like harnesslooms. Those under the age of 11 were involved in activities such as filling prints or bobbins, commonly referred to as winding, with weekly wages amounting to 2/- in the 1850s. It was not uncommon for children to work in these capacities after their regular school hours. In Renfrew, draw boys earned varying wages, ranging from 1/6d to 2/6d per week during the 1830s and 1840s. Meanwhile, in Paisley, draw boys, typically above the age of 12, were paid wages amounting to 5/- in the 1850s.[3] In the print work industry, prevalent in nearly all the parishes of the county, children were employed as tearers, assisting block printers in the process of calico printing.

In Paisley's shawl warehouse and calendar works, a few girls under the age of 11 were employed as sewers and finishers of shawls. Local factory inspectors observed that, in the same town where there were regulations for employment in spinning mills, the availability of print work employment led to print work being considered an alternative for child labor. An illustrative case in Paisley involved an owner objecting to a child working 12 hours, only to be told, "Oh, never mind, she can go to a print field until she is old enough."[4] After the age of 13, girls could earn more money in mills. As boy tearers aged, they found fewer opportunities in the textile industry. Apart from textiles, boys also worked in iron foundries, sugar works, and assisted carpenters in the shipbuilding industry. In sugar works and carpentry, where boys were typically above 13 years old, wages ranged from 5–6d. a week in the 1830s and 1840s. The data from 1871 shows various jobs employing children aged 10-15, with some below the age of 10 (Table LIX).

Table LVIX:

No. of children of the age group of 10–15 (with a small number under 10 years) employed in different works and services in Renfrewshire in 1871

Serial no.	Name of the occupations	No. of children (8–15)
1.	Manufactures: silk, carpet, woolen, and muslin	361
	Cotton and thread	994
2.	In building industries as plasterers, masons, carvers, and joiners	228
3.	Iron, wooden ship, and boat building	136
4.	Textile factories	775
5.	Weaving	257
6.	Calico printing, dressmaking, tailoring, shoemaking	699
7.	Hawkers, newspaper agents, harbor warehouse workers, and different machine factories	321
8.	Sugar refineries, coal mines, iron mines, mine borers, stone courier	491
9.	Commercial clerk	102
10.	Messers port errand	597
11.	Boiler workers, blacksmiths, general laborers, and factories branches not mentioned	567
	Total	5,600

Source: *Census of Scotland, 1871, Vol. 11, 365–68.*

Children under the age of 13 engaged in employment were required to present a certificate from teachers confirming their school attendance for a specific minimum number of hours. Despite this requirement, mill owners displayed no concern for the education of the working children. A factory inspector remarked that the owners exhibited:

> an unwillingness to take even that moderate degree of trouble which would have been sufficient to ensure an improvement in the moral condition of the children by

attendance at school and have followed the easier course to themselves of dismissing all under 12 years of age.[5]

Despite attempts to regulate child labor, opportunities for child wage labor endured, and a substantial number of children were engaged in employment before reaching the age of 13 in the mid-19th century. The register general's report in 1851 highlighted that:

> children of the laboring classes are employed at an early age, some permanently, others temporarily... Even the lowest amount of wages... from 1 to 6d, to 2 and unavailable week must be so great a relief to the parents as to render it almost hopeless that they can withstand the inducement and retain the child at school in the face of such temptation.[6]

Reverend Macfarlane of Renfrew parish expressed that "parents were compelled to send their children to work at around seven to eight years of age, halting their educational progress just when they had barely begun."[7]

In rural regions, both boys and girls assisted their parents during the harvest season by harvesting potatoes, and turnips, gathering vegetables, and transporting meals to the fields, among other tasks. Additionally, they supported their fathers in plowing and sowing seeds during other periods, typically after attending school or on weekends. In dairy farming areas, children contributed to feeding livestock, including cattle and sheep, and participated in milking cows. Boys were also employed as farm servants for wages on various farms.

There were variations in child labor among the migrant and the local-born. The opportunity for child labor might have influenced the family migration pattern to different parts of the county. The Irish were more numerous in Paisley, Greenock, Port Glasgow, Neilston, and Mearns, where there were openings for children to work. There were migrants from other parts of Scotland and the Highlands, whose children were also working. Table LX shows the percentage of children employed in textiles (non-hand-weaving) in Paisley among different groups of people.

Table LX:
Percentage of the selected age groups of children in textile employment (non-hand-weaving), Paisley 1851 (no. in brackets)

Age	Migrant		Non-Migrants
	Irish	Scots	
9–10	12(6)	6(2)	13(13)
11–12	53(26)	28(8)	37(13)
13–14	60(31)	39(10)	67(14)

Source: Table 7.8, Brenda Collins, op. cit., 161.

Among 9 and 10-year-olds, the percentage of children employed in the non-hand-weaving sector was nearly identical between Irish migrants and non-migrants. However, when considering different age groups collectively, a higher number of children of Irish origin were engaged in employment. This was primarily due to the necessity for children to contribute to family income. In some instances, the inability to afford school fees led to child labor. The 1843 Parliamentary Report aptly captured the situation, noting, "the desire of parents to make something by the children's work and also perhaps the convenience of being able to send them out of the way and where they are kept in safety during the day was a great temptation."[8]

6.3 Population Expansion and Economic Depression Causing Regional Variation Absences

Between 1830 and 1870, there was a significant increase in the population of urban areas across the country, leading to an impact on existing educational facilities. The proportion of children attending schools in relation to the total population varied from town to town, village to village, and parish to parish (refer to Table LXI).

Table LXI:
Population and scholars in different towns, villages, and the parish as a whole in 1871 in Renfrewshire (age group 5–13 years)

Name of the parish	Town area			Village area					
	Total pop.	Scholars	% of scholars out of total pop.	Total pop.	Scholars	%	Total pop.	Scholars	%
Abbey Paisley	7,640	1,036	13.00	3,232	628	19.45	17,489	2,351	13.44
Cathcart	220	16	7.27	2,737	407	14.87	7,134	1,041	14.64
Eaglesham	-	-	-	1,237	172	13.9	1,714	227	13.24
Eastwood	11,044	1,802	16.32	626	116	18.53	12,933	1,947	15.02
Erskine	-	-	-	323	63	19.5	1,565	251	16.04
Greenock	58,877	7,415	12.61	-	-	-	58,817	7,415	12.61

Name of the parish	Town area			Village area					
	Total pop.	Scholars	% of scholars out of total pop.	Total pop.	Scholars	%	Total pop.	Scholars	%
Houston & Killellan	-	-	-	1,547	193	12.5	2,167	273	12.6
Inchinan	-	-	-	-	-	-	584	85	14.73
Inverkip	-	-	-	-	-	-	937	135	14.41
Gourock	2,946	422	14.35	-	-	-	3,291	471	14.31
Kilbarchan	2,678	381	14.23	2,710	379	14.00	6,093	806	13.23
Kilmalcom	-	-	-	-	-	-	1,716	223	13.00
Lochwinnoch	-	-	-	1,995	270	13.53	3,816	466	12.21
Mearns	1,401	193	13.78	775	104	13.42	3,543	452	12.76
Neilston	5,807	693	11.0	3,005	387	12.88	11,136	1,352	12.15
Paisley	48,257	6,614	13.71	-	-	-	48,257	6,614	13.71
Port Glasgow	10,823	1,589	14.68	-	-	-	10,823	1,589	14.68
Renfrew	4,163	547	13.14	-	-	-	4,163	547	13.14

Source: Census of Scotland 1871, vol. II, ex/vii.

In rural areas, a higher percentage of children attended schools compared to urban areas. Due to the absence of precise data on the proportion of children in the total population, definitive conclusions regarding area-wide variations cannot be drawn. Discrepancies in the number of children between different areas may exist. Nonetheless, data for the entire Renfrewshire, as well as for the towns of Paisley and Greenock, is available for the year 1871, indicating that nearly two out of five children, or 36.78%, in the 5–15 years age group were not enrolled in school (refer to Table LXIII). It is important to note that during that period, the majority of scholars typically commenced schooling around five or six years old and concluded by the age of nine or ten, with only a few continuing up to 14 or 15 years. Historical records suggest that some children completed whatever education they received in one or two years. Therefore, it can be inferred that 37% of children not on the school roll might possess basic literacy. The school board's second Annual Report of 1875 stated that, in 1871, there were 39,939 children in Renfrewshire in the age group 5–13, of which 26,095 (65%) were receiving education.[9]

Table LXII:

Percentage of children attending schools out of the total children in Paisley, Greenock, and Renfrewshire as a whole between the age group of 5–15 in 1871.

Parish county	Pupils in attendance (5–15)	Total children (5–15)	%
Paisley	7,055	11,102	63.55
Greenock	8,435	12,881	65.48
Renfrewshire (entire county including Paisley & Greenock)	28,082	44,420	63.22

Source: *Educational Statistics, Census a/Scotland, 1871, Vol. II ex/vi.*

A comparable pattern of school attendance among children was evident in Ayrshire and Lanarkshire, as illustrated in Table LXIII. The average attendance rate for the entire country of Scotland was higher. Notably, the figures for Aberdeen and Edinburgh indicated considerably greater school attendance compared to Greenock and Paisley. The lower attendance rates in these industrial areas, including Renfrewshire, may be attributed to the population surge and substantial immigration, particularly from Ireland.

Table LXIII:

Percentage of children attending schools out of the total children in some towns and counties in Scotland in the age group of 5–15 in 1871

Area	Pupils in attendance (5–15)	Total children (5–15)	%
Glasgow	60,649	100,691	60.23
Edinburgh	30,433	39,624	76.80
Aberdeen	15,036	10,386	77.36
Ayrshire	33,019	50,181	65.80
Lanarkshire	10,157	171,882	61.93
Stirlingshire	15,939	23,178	68.77
Scotland	541,995	775,871	69.77

Source: *Educational Statistics, Census of Scotland 1871, Vol. II ex/vii.*

Migration, particularly from Ayrshire and neighboring counties, significantly contributed to the population surge in urban areas of Renfrewshire. Migrant groups, sharing similar backgrounds with the local population, prioritized the education of their children. This commitment to education extended to migrants from the Scottish Highlands, with Reverend Macfarlane of the Gaelic church in Greenock actively advocating for education in the 1840s. Notably, individuals of Highland origin played crucial roles in the educational landscape, exemplified by Duncan A. Campbell's pivotal role in establishing the Greenock Academy. The institution later established the Campbell Prize in 1863.[10] Unfortunately, there is no statistical evidence indicating whether a higher percentage of Highland children attended school compared to other groups in Greenock. However, many

Highland children availed themselves of the educational opportunities. The percentage of Highlanders unable to write was roughly similar to that of local-born individuals or migrants from other parts of Renfrewshire. Comparatively, individuals migrating from the Lowlands and England had better literacy rates (see Table LXIV). In a specific area of Paisley in 1851, school attendance was nearly identical among Highland and other children (those born in Paisley, Renfrewshire, or Lowland counties; see Table LXV).

Table LXIV:

Highland groups and locals born in Greenock signing the marriage register by marks in 1851

	Men	Women	Total
Inhabitants of Greenock (born in Highlands) - H	13.4	24.0	37.4
Inhabitants of Greenock (born in the county of Bute)-B	0.0	0.0	0.0
Inhabitants of Greenock (born in Greenock) - G	11.1	20.15	31.16
Inhabitants of Greenock (born in Renfrew) - R	14.8	25.0	39.8
Inhabitants of Greenock (born in Lowlands) - L	1.9	17.7	18.16
Inhabitants of Greenock (born in Ireland) - 1	53.3	75.6	128.9
Inhabitants of Greenock (counties other than Scotland) - E	11.4	8.3	19.7
Total population	105.9	172.1	275.12

Source: Lobban, op. cit., 491, Table 51.

Table LXV:

Percentage of children in the age group of 5-11, attending school in a particular area in 1851 in Paisley

Highlanders	57.7%
Irish	51.9%
Remainder of population	56.8%
The population of that particular area of Paisley (5–11) as a whole	56.3%

Sources: Census Enumeration Book, Paisley, 1851, Table XIVA, D. Doherty, op. cit.

The Irish, comprising a significant portion of immigrants, faced challenges in providing education for their children, primarily due to financial constraints. Unfortunately, there is no specific statistical evidence available for the entire Renfrewshire regarding the attendance of Irish children in schools. However, local data highlights the education challenges and the relatively lower school attendance rate among the Irish in a specific area of Paisley in 1851 (see Table LXVI). Additionally, there were instances of Irish children being classified as vagrants, with a police report in 1871 indicating that 225 vagrant children picked up in Paisley were all of Irish origin. In times of unemployment, some Irish families resorted to sending their children to beg for support (see Table LXV).[11]

In Paisley and Kilbarchan, a notable challenge was the education of the children of weavers. Historically, weavers were often knowledgeable, upstanding, and exemplary individuals.[12] However, by the mid-19th century, financial hardships had rendered many weavers practically unable to afford education for their children. The 1833 Parliamentary Report highlighted a decline in the number of children receiving formal instruction in basic learning principles. Subsequent findings revealed that several draw boys in Paisley were unable to write, and their reading proficiency was limited to the New Testament. This deteriorating state of education was prevalent among the children of weavers in various weaving centers in western Scotland. Faced with destitution, these families struggled to afford school fees, which were 1/- per month for each child, while fees in larger towns were relatively higher, at 4/- per quarter in the 1830s.[13] In 1863, a weaver's wife in Paisley lamented, "I have five children, but they are unable to attend school due to the inability to pay the 2d. a week. Instead, I send them to Sunday school, which provides them with a bit of learning."[14]

For the majority of Scottish weavers and other working children, the primary avenue for acquiring basic numeracy and literacy was through Sunday schools, where instruction was often offered without charge. However, in Paisley, these schools were deemed inadequate for imparting fundamental knowledge. They primarily assisted those who had already acquired some reading skills, with a focus on teaching the Bible. A few working children also attended evening schools, yet concerns lingered regarding the extent of their benefit from these classes after a day of labor lasting 10–12 hours at the loom and in other occupations.[15] Among the enrolled children, a portion of them were not actively participating in school attendance (see Table LXVI). Once more, rural regions demonstrated a superior attendance percentage compared to urban areas, albeit with some exceptions. Inchinan, for instance, reported a full attendance of 100%. The rural areas did not experience the same population surge as the urban centers.

Table LXVI:

No. of scholars attending schools out of the total pupils in Renfrewshire in 1865 outside Paisley, Greenock, and a portion of Abbey Paisley

Parish	Children present	Children on roll	%
Abbey (Paisley)	607	797	76.16
Cathcart	238	313	76.04
Eaglesham	240	295	81.36
Eastwood	1326	1663	79.74
Erskine	176	201	87.56
Gourock	210	228	92.11
Houston and Killellan	395	549	71.95
Inchinan	110	110	100.0

Parish	Children present	Children on roll	%
Inverkip	186	208	89.42
Kilbarchan	478	670	71.34
Kilmacolm	133	162	82.1
Lochwinnock	445	561	79.3
Mearns	473	599	78.96
Neilston	852	1142	74.4
Port Glasgow	716	1132	63.25
Renfrew	632	773	81.76

Source: PP 1867xxvi, 212–17.

In certain locations, the population was diminished due to outward migration. Children in these regions served as farmhands and assisted their parents in the fields during harvest, coinciding with the closure of schools. Additionally, the fees in rural parish schools were more affordable (the lowest being in Inchinan, 1/- for English, 1/4d. for arithmetic in 1837) compared to town parishes. Gourock exhibited a commendable attendance record, attributed to its nature as a sea resort rather than an industrial town, with a concentration of middle-class residents explaining this phenomenon.

The predominant cause of absenteeism in urban parishes likely stemmed from the allure of child labor. Although many might have initially enrolled, financial challenges hindered their ability to persist. These scholars were likely compelled to contribute to their family's income, prompting them to discontinue their education. Some students may have attended school intermittently, balancing periods of education with work throughout the year. This indicates an awareness among the community about the importance of children's education, but economic constraints or insufficient income forced parents to withdraw their children from school.

6.4 Conclusion

Child labor opportunities were abundant for those aged 11–13, despite the state's increasing involvement in educating impoverished children through factory legislation. Renfrewshire saw the employment of children under 10, particularly from Irish backgrounds, which affected their education. Town areas faced challenges due to population growth, impacting educational facilities, while rural regions showed higher percentages of school attendance relative to the total population. The surge in population, driven by Irish migrants, resulted in lower school attendance percentages among them due to lower income. The weavers in Paisley, once esteemed, struggled to educate their children in the 1840s and 1850s. Town areas experienced a more acute problem than rural ones, primarily due to child labor and economic conditions. Although parents were willing to send their children to school, financial difficulties often forced them to withdraw.

Chapter 7: Conclusion

The changes in social structure had a significant impact on education in Renfrewshire. The increase in population in urban areas threatened the educational facilities available and put a strain on the traditional structure. From 1830 to 1870, there was a decline in the Church of Scotland's influence in education due to the Disruption of 1843 and the middle classes' demand for state control in education. State inspection replaced the Presbyterian inspection of schools in the 1840s, but the inspection remained denominational. The Education Act of 1861 ended the connection between the parish school and the Church of Scotland, which opened the office of the parish master to teachers of other denominations. Although it is unclear whether there was a definite increase in the number of schools run by the Church of Scotland, it is evident that there was a rise in the number of scholars in parish schools in proportion to the population expansion. Between 1862 and 1865, 32% of pupils attended these schools in areas outside Paisley and Greenock, while in these two towns in 1854, 21% of pupils were in church schools. Thus, a larger proportion of scholars were attending other types of schools.

In the 1840s, the Free Church challenged the position where the Established Church provided most schools. As a result, the Free Church established its own school system in Scotland. Although the Free Church erected some of the best schools in some parishes of Renfrewshire, financial difficulties prevented them from building schools in many other parishes. Therefore, the provision of Free Church schools was eventually patchy. Although the initiative of the Free Church led to an increase in the number of schools and school places, only 8.39% of the scholars were attending these church schools between 1862–65, in the county (outside Paisley and Greenock). Data from 1854 show that 11.1% of pupils in Greenock and Paisley were attending Free Church schools.

Another factor that affected education was mainly the migration of the Catholic Irish. The Catholic church made valiant efforts to deal with its followers' education problem. From the data available, it appears that there was a rise in the number of scholars in these church schools in proportion to the expansion of the Catholic population. Despite its financial difficulties, the church provided education to 12% of the scholars between 1862 and 1865 (outside Paisley and Greenock). In 1857, Catholic schools had a 5% share of pupils in Paisley and Greenock. The Episcopal church also had a few schools in Renfrewshire.

During the time when churches were responsible for providing education, they were unable to cater to all children. As a result, private institutions such as subscription and adventure schools emerged, primarily in urban areas. However, available evidence suggests that the number of these schools decreased in certain regions during the period being studied, particularly in rural areas. Most students who attended these schools were from low-income families, and the fees charged were generally lower than those of parish and church schools, except for Catholic schools. In Renfrewshire outside of Paisley and Greenock, 40% of all scholars on the roll between 1862-65 came from subscription and adventure schools. In Paisley, almost 47% of scholars attended these schools in 1854, which was nearly half of the student population.

Some efforts were also made by the town councils in the burghs to provide school places, which children of the middle-income group mainly took with a few poor scholars. Another key feature of the period was the increased role played by the state. The legislation of 1803 and 1838 increased the number of schools which the heritors had to provide. The state started the grant system through inspection from the 1840s. At first, the grant was provided for erecting school buildings, books, and equipment. Grants for certificated and pupil-teachers were introduced in 1846. All grants were lumped into one grant in 1862 and were awarded on the basis of the performance of the students in the three Rs: reading, writing, and arithmetic. Renfrewshire received a proportional amount from the state. Despite the rosy picture suggested by the efforts of different bodies, things were far from perfect. There was a lack of central control and compulsion.

It is difficult to assess whether there was an overall increase in the number of schools during the period under study, as 66 schools out of 177 (more than one third) failed to provide information, though there was complete data of parish, burgh, and Catholic church schools. But if a tentative conclusion can be made, it would appear that school places almost kept pace with the expansion of population. A comparison with the rise of population between 1837–72 produces a proportionately higher rise in the number of scholars. There was a 33% increase in population in the county between 1831 and 1861. Corresponding available data reveals the rise in the number of scholars in 28 parishes between 1837–65 (Paisley and Greenock, between 1837–54) was nearly four times higher.

It is hard to determine the quality of educational facilities in Renfrewshire. However, in 1861–62, one quarter of the teachers had received formal training. They either completed a two-year program at the Free Church normal schools in Glasgow and Edinburgh or they received a certificate after their first year of training from church training schools in Edinburgh and Glasgow. The number of Catholic trained teachers was low, as only one out of fourteen in Renfrewshire had received formal training, due to the lack of training facilities for them in Scotland.

The standard of education, judged by the curriculum followed and number of trained teachers in some of the different church and subscription schools, was satisfactory in the contemporary view as evidenced by the reports of the government inspections. In a number of subscription, Catholic, and almost all the adventure schools, standards were ill-equipped for good education. However, without these schools, a vast proportion of children would remain out of any formal education and their contribution cannot be denied.

During the time of industrialization, the educational system did not entirely collapse, but the negative effects of the economic change were evident in the form of non-attendance. Children in rural areas had a slightly better attendance rate because they could work for their parents during the harvest holiday. However, absenteeism was high among Catholic children and those residing in urban areas due to child wage labor. Although there were regulations regarding the age for commencing work from the 1840s in Scotland, parents often evaded them. Additionally, certain textile-related work did not come under these regulations. As a result, in 1871, 35% of children in Renfrewshire County aged between 5–13 were not on any school roll. This included those who had left school for jobs after two or three years of schooling at the age of 9 or 10. The majority of the children tended to leave school between the ages of 9 and 11.

Renfrewshire was quite similar to other industrial counties in Lowland Scotland, such as Ayrshire, Stirlingshire, and Lanarkshire.

However, in Ayrshire, the Established and Free Churches were more active in establishing schools. On the other hand, the Roman Catholic Church was more effective in Renfrewshire than in Lanarkshire, which is a concentrated area of Catholics. In Renfrewshire and Stirlingshire, adventure and subscription schools had a more prominent role than Ayrshire. Additionally, the number of children on school rolls was identical in industrial areas of Lowland Scotland with a large number of Irish immigrants.

Bibliography

1.   PRIMARY MATERIAL

Census Enumeration Book, 1851, Greenock.

Census Enumeration Book 1851, Kilmacolm.

Census Preamble, 1851, Paisley.

Census Enumeration Schedule N.R.H.1851, Paisley Vol. 460–475.

Registers of Civil Registered Marriage, 1855, Paisley, 559/1–3, 573/1–3.

Roman Catholic Parish Register, Paisley, RII/21/81/1-0.

2.   PARLIAMENTARY PAPERS, MINUTES AND REPORTS

a)   Parliamentary Papers

1834 x, Select Committee on Handloom Weavers.

1836 xlvi, Factory Inspectors Reports, Leonard Homer.

1839 (159) xiii, Handloom Weavers, Scotland, and Continental Europe.

1839 xiii, Factory Inspectors Report, Return of Mills and Factories.

1839 xiii, Dr. Harding's Report and Mr. Symons Report.

1841 x, Factory Inspectors Report.

1841 xix, Answers made by schoolmasters in Scotland to queries circulated in 1838, by order of the Select Committee on Education in Scotland, part one - School not parochial and Part 11 - Parochial schools.

1843 vii, Report on Distress (Paisley) Sel. cttee., Minutes of Evidence.

1843 xv (432), Children's Employment Commission (Trades and Manufactures) Appendix to Second Report pt. 11.

1843 xvi, Children's Employment Commission, First Report (Mines) Appendix Part I.

1843 xxii - 1841 Census Enumeration Abstract.

1852 liii, Return Relating to Heritors and Commissioners of Supply, Commission of Supply.

PP *1854 lix* - Return to an Addition of the House of Commons, 13th Feb., 1854.

1854/5, xii, 316 - Return showing the total amount of Educational Grants from the Privy Council to each county in Scotland, from 1833 to 1855, distinguishing the object of the Grant and the religious denomination to which it was paid.

1857/8 xlvi, Returns for the years 1854, 1855 and 1856 respectively, of the Names of the Parishes in each county in Scotland within whose Bounds any School is situated, in respect of which any money has been paid under the authority of the Committee of Council on Education, stating the number of such schools in each Parish, and the names of the places in each Parish in which such schools are situated and the religious body to which each is connected, distinguishing the Parochial schools from other schools connected with the Established Church and specifying the amount paid to each school in each year.

1862 xliii, Return of number of schools (other than burgh school or school within a royal burgh and other than adventure schools) in every parish in Scotland stating the area of each parish, distance of schools in each parish from each other and specifying the description of each school, whether parochial or connected with any committee, society or Religious Denominations and also number of pupils in ordinary attendance at every such school at the date of return.

1863 xlvi, Return of the amount paid to each Parish or Place in 1860–61, under the Heads of Grants to Certificated Teachers, Assistant or Probationary Teachers, Pupil Teachers and Gratuities to masters and mistresses and capitation grants and the total amount of all such Grants paid to each parish or place.

1863 xlvi, Return of Amount of Subscription, donations and collections in places of worship or elsewhere received in 1860–61 by each school aided by grants from Privy Council.

1863 xlvi, Return of Total Amount of School salary payable by Landward Heritors, in every parish, under Act 43 Geo 3, c54, as at the date of passing of the Act 24 and 25 Vict c 107. Total amount of the addition made to such salary under the last mentioned act, including allowance to Female Teachers. Of the total amount of Annual Grants from the Committee of Council on Education in 1861 to schools in every parish distinguishing (1) parochial schools (2) schools within the Burgh and (3) other schools.

1864 xxii, Children's Employment, Trade and Manufacture, Second Report with Appendix.

1865 xvii, Education (Scotland) Commission, First Report, (also known as Argyle Commission) A.C.I. 1865, Minutes of Evidence.

1867 xxv (3858) Appendix to First Report.

1867 xxvi (3845-v) Statistics relative to schools in Scotland.

1867 xxv (3845), Second Report, with an Appendix, A.C.II. 1867. Elementary schools.

1867 xxv (3845-iv) Report on the state of Education in the Hebrides, by Alexander Nicolson, 1866.

1867/8 xxix (4011) A.C.III, vol. I, Burgh and middle-class schools, together with the General Report of the Assistant Commissioners, 1868.

1867/8 xxix (4011-1) A.C. Ill, vol. 11, Special Reports of the Assistant Commissioners on Burgh and middle-class schools, 1868.

1867/8 xxviii pt. v (3966-v) Schools Enquiry Commission, Report on certain Burgh schools and other schools of Secondary Education in Scotland, D.R. Fearon, 1868.

1874, xvii, Second Report, Endowed Schools and Hospitals (Scotland) Commission.

1884 xxxii-vi, (3980) Report of the Commission of Enquiry into the condition of the crofters and cottars in the Highlands and Islands of Scotland with evidence and appen-dices.

1886 xxviii (4664), Second Report Endowed Schools and Hospitals (Scotland) Commission.

1887 lxxxix (5172). Return relating to wages [giving particulars of the rates paid to different classes of workers in the various industries in different districts of the United Kingdom, during many years prior to 1850, 1855 and in subsequent years].

(b) Minutes and Reports

Address from the Presbytery of Paisley to Friends etc., April 1837.

Board of Education for Scotland, Second Report 1875.

C.C.M Committee of Council on Education in Scotland, Minutes and Reports, 1839-1939.

1843/4, Part 11, Gibson, J., Report on Schools in Scotland.

1845, Part 11, Gordon, J., On the State of Education in the counties of Stirling, Clackmannan, Linlithgow and Renfrew.

1850/51, E. Woodford, General Reports on Schools Inspection.

1854/5, E. Woodford, General Reports on Schools Inspected.

1856/7, J. Gordon, On Schools Inspected in the West of Scotland.

1857/8, J. Gordon, On Schools Inspected in the South Western Division of Scotland.

1858/9, Wilson, C.E., On Schools Inspected in the West of Scotland.

1866/7, Wilson, C.E., On Schools inspected in the West of Scotland and in the Western Isles.

1871/2, Gordon, J., On Schools Inspected in the Counties of Edinburgh, Haddington, Linlithgow, Peebles, Selkirk, Roxburgh and Berwick.

Census of Great Britain, 1831, vol. II

Census of Great Britain, 1841, vol. II

Census of Great Britain, 1851, vol. II

Census of Scotland, 1861, vol. II

Census of Scotland, 1871, vol. II

1872/3, Middleton, D. Schools inspected in the counties of Lanark and Renfrew.

Educational Committee Report, General Assembly of the Church of Scotland, 1844, 1851.

Free Church Minute, 5th Feb., 1872.

Lawrie, S.S., Report on Education in the Parochial Schools of the Counties of Aberdeen, Banff and Moray, addressed to the Trustees of the Dick Bequest, Edinburgh 1890.

Lewis, J. Cornwallis, *The Report on the State of the Irish Poor in Great Britain,* 1843.

Mann, H., *Report for 1843,* Boston, 1865.

Proceedings of the General Assembly of the Free Church of Scotland, Oct., 1843.

3. OTHER REPORTS

Annual Report, Paisley Industrial School.

Greenock Town Council Report.

4. NEWSPAPERS

Greenock Advertiser, April 23, 1859.

The Times, 18th June, 1839.

Strong, J., Social and Economic Statistics of Glasgow, 1851-61, *Glasgow Herald,* Shipbuilding and Engineering Greenock Advertiser, April 23, Supplement.

Thomson, J.G., 'The County Authority of Renfrewshire', *The Educational News,* March 14th 1903.

5. JOURNALS

Bowley, A.L., 'Statistics of Wages with United Kingdom during the last hundred years, agricultural wages', *Journal of the Royal Statistical Society,* 1899.

Clark, E.A. 'The Superiority of the Scotch System, Scottish Ragged Schools and their influence', *Scottish Educational Studies,* Vol. 9 no. 7, May 1977.

Dillon, T., 'The Irish in Leeds I 851-61,' *Thorsely Society Publication* LIV pt. I.

Richard, C.R., Irish Settlement in nineteenth century Bradford', *Yorkshire Bulletin of Economic and Social Research,* 1968, xx.

Knox, J., 'An Old Educational Reformer', *Scottish Educational Journal,* No. 20, 1953.

Myers, J.D., "Scottish Nationalism and the Antecedents of the 1872 Education Act', *Scottish Educational Studies,* vol. 4, no. 2, Nov. 1972.

Osborne, R.H., 'The Movement of People in Scotland', 1851- 1951 ', *Scottish Studies*, vol. II, 1958.

Anonymous, Greenock Academy, Scottish Country Life, April 1921 [then united with the Scottish Motor Transport Magazine].

6. UNPUBLISHED THESIS

Collins, B.E.A., 'Aspects of Irish Immigration into Two Scottish Towns (Dundee and Paisley) during the mid-nineteenth century', (M. Phil 1. thesis, Edinburgh University), 1979.

Cooper, C., 'The Development of Education in the burgh of Greenock, with particular reference to the period of the First Five Boards 1873–88', (M.Ed. Thesis, Glasgow University), 1969.

Doherty, D., 'The Migration of Highlanders into Lowland Scotland 1780–1850, with particular reference to Paisley: (Honours dissertation, Strathclyde University) I 976–7.

Lobban, R.D., 'The Migration of Highlanders into Lowland Scotland, 1750–1850, with particular reference to Greenock', (Ph.D. thesis, Edinburgh University), 1969.

Monies, M., 'The Impact of the 1972 Education (Scotland) Act on Scottish Working Class Education up to 1899', (Ph.D. thesis, Edinburgh University) 1974.

Nisbet, C., 'A Short Study in Social and Economic History in the County of Renfrewshire: c. 1800–1850', (Honours dissertation, Economic History, Strathclyde University) 1971/2.

White, D.D., 'The Handloom Weavers in Glasgow and Paisley and their relationship with Chartism 1838–42'. (Honours dissertation, Economic History, Strathclyde University) 1976/7.

7.   BOOKS

Anderson, M., *Family Structure in Nineteenth Century Lancashire*, (Cambridge, 1971).

Aird, A., *Glimpses of Old Glasgow*, (Glasgow 1894).

Bain, A., *Education in Stirlingshire*, (London, 1965).

Blair, M., *The Paisley Thread Industry*, (Paisley, 1907).

Bone, T.R., *School Inspection in Scotland 1840–1966*, (Edin-burgh, 1968).

Boyd, W., *Education in Ayrshire through Seven Centuries*, (Edinburgh, 1961).

Brown, R., *History of Paisley, vol. I and II*, (Paisley, 1886).

Brown, R., *History of Paisley Grammar School*, (Paisley, 1875).

Buchanan, R., *The Ten Years Conflict*, (Glasgow, 1852).

Clarke, J., *Short Studies in Education in Scotland*, (Longmans, 1904).

Cleland, J., *Enumeration of the Inhabitants of Glasgow, and its connected suburbs, together with population and statistical tables relative to Scotland and England*, (Glasgow 1820).

Cumming, J.E., *The Church of Scotland, vol. vii* (Edinburgh, 1871).

Drummond, A.L. and Bullock, J., *The Church in Victorian Scot-land 1843–74,* (Edinburgh, 1975).

Gray, M., *The Highland Economy 1750–1850,* (Oliver and Boyd, 1951).

Habakkuk, H.J., *American and British Technology in the Nine-teenth Century,* (Cambridge, 1962).

Handley, J.E., *The Irish in Scotland 1798–1845,* (Glasgow, 1945).

Hamilton, H., *The Industrial Revolution in Scotland,* (Oxford, 1932).

Howard, R.C., *The Weavers Cottage, Kilbarchan,* National Trust Publications, (Edinburgh, 1962).

Hutchins, B.L. and Harrison, A., *History of the Factory Legislation,* (London, 1903).

Jessop, J.C., *Education in Angus,* (Edinburgh 1931).

Kerr, J., *Memories Grave and Gay,* (Nelson n.d. 1905).

Kerr, J., *Scottish Education, School and University from early times to 1908,* (Cambridge, 1913).

Knox, H.M. *Two Hundred and Fifty Years of Scottish Education 1696–1946,* (Oliver and Boyd, 1953).

Lythe, S.G.E. and Butt, J., *An Economic History of Scotland,* (Glasgow, 1975).

MacCarthur, F., *History of Port Glasgow,* (Glasgow, 1932).

MacDonald, D.F., *Scotland's Shifting Population,* (Jackson, 1937).

MacLaren, *Religion and Social Class,* (London, 1974).

MacKenzie, R.D. Rev., *Kilbarchan, A Parish History,* (Paisley, 1902).

McCarthy, M., *A Social Geography of Paisley,* (Paisley, 1969).

Metcalfe, William, M., *History of Paisley,* (Paisley, 1909).

Mitchison, R., *A History of Scotland,* (London, 1970).

Mort, F., *Renfrewshire,* (Cambridge, 1912).

Murray, D., *Memories of the Old College of Glasgow, Some Chapters in the History of the University* (Glasgow, 1927).

Murray, D., *Reminiscences of Sixty Years in the History of Paisley,* (Paisley, 1875).

Murray, N., *A Social History of the Scottish Handloom Weavers 1790–1850,* (Edinburgh, 1976).

New Statistical Accounts, Vol. VII, (Edinburgh, 1845).

Parkhill, J., *History of Paisley,* (Paisley, 1857).

Paton, J.G., *Autobiography,* (London, 1891).

Porter, G.R., *Progress of the Nation,* (London, 1851).

Pride, D., *History of the Parish of Neilston* (Paisley, 1910).

Saunders, J., *Scottish Democracy, 1815–40,* (Edinburgh, 1950).

Scotland, J., *The History of Scottish Education,* vol. I, (London, 1969).

Skinnidar, M., 'Catholic Elementary Education in Glasgow 1818–1918', *Studies in the History of Scottish Education 1872–1939',* T.R. Bone edited, (London, 1967).

Slaven, A., *The Development of the West of Scotland 1750–1960,* (London, 1975).

Smith, R.M., *History of Greenock,* (Greenock, 1921).

Smout, T.C., 'The Strange Intervention of Edward Twistleton, Paisley in Depression, 1841-3', *The Search for Wealth and Stability,* Edited by T.C. Smout, (London, 1979).

Stow, D., *The Training System of Education, Religious, Intellectual and Moral, as Established in the Glasgow Normal Training Seminary,* (Blackie, 1845).

Thatcher, B.M., 'The Episcopal Church in Helensburgh', *Scottish Themes,* edited by J. Butt and T. Ward, (Edinburgh, 1976).

Third Statistical Account, The County of Renfrew and Bute, (Ed-inburgh, 1962).

Wallace, J., *Observations on the causes of the Great Mortality in Greenock,* (Greenock, 1860).

Walker, N.L., *Chapters from the History of the Free Church of Scotland,* (Edinburgh, 1895).

Wilson, J., *Tales and Travels of a School Inspector,* (Glasgow, 1928).

8. OTHER REFERENCES

Beale, J.M. A History of the Burgh and Parochial Schools in Fife, from Reformation to 1872, (unpublished Ph.D. thesis, Edinburgh, University, 1953).

Boyd, S.A., *Old Days and Ways in Newton Mearns,* (Glasgow, 1939).

Craigie, J., *A Bibliography of Scottish Education before 1872,* (London, 1970).

Ferguson, W., *Scotland 1689 to the Present,* (Oliver and Boyd, 1968).

Frairley, J.A., 'Beginning of the Compulsory Education in Scotland 1872-1883', (unpublished M. ed. thesis, Glasgow University, 1965).

Gilmour, D., *Paisley Weavers of other days,* (London, 1876).

Harvie, C., *Scotland and Nationalism,* (London, 1977).

Johnson, R., 'Really useful knowledge', *Working Class Culture,* edited by Clarke, Chritcher and Johnson, (London, 1979).

Macdonald, C.G., *Inverkip 1798–1858,* (Greenock, 1946).

Mackintosh, M., *Education in Scotland Yesterday and Today,* (Glasgow, 1962).

Mcbilion, J., 'Catholic Education in Ayr, 1823–1918', *Innes Review.*

Metcalf, W.M., *A History of the County of Renfrew* (Paisley, 1905).

Ross, W. Rev., *Busby and its neighbourhood,* (Edinburgh, 1883).

Rusk, R.R., *The Training of Teachers in Scotland,* (Edinburgh, 1928).

Scottish Industrial History, A Miscellany, (Edinburgh, 1978).

Simon, B., *Studies in the History of Education,* 1780–1870, (London, 1960).

Smith, R.M., *A Page of Local History,* (Greenock, 1904).

The Statistical Account of Scotland, (Edinburgh, 1791–9).

Treble, J.H., 'The development of Roman Catholic education in Scotland 1878–1978', *The Innes Review,* vol. xxix, 2.

Weir, D., *History of the Town of Greenock,* (Greenock, 1829).

Williamson, G., *Old Greenock,* (Paisley, 1888).

West, E.G., *Education and the Industrial Revolution* (London, 1975).

Appendix

Table-I: Summary of information on schools in Renfrewshire [Except Greenock and Paisley I in 1865, based on type of school]

Type of School	No. of schools	No. of students on rolls	No. of students present	Percentage of students on roll present in school	Percentage of total no. of students on roll	Percentage of total no. of students actually present	Percentage of students on roll for Scotland
Parochial	13	1761	1483	84.21	18.73	20.56	24.4
Free Church	9	842	671	79.69	8.95	9.3	15.6
Church of Scotland	7	723	546	75.52	7.69	7.57	10.6
Subscriptional undenominational & factory School	38	3185	2444	76.73	33.86	33.89	29.3
Roman Catholic	8	911	410	45	9.69	6.95	1.8
Private adventure	18	676	534	79	7.19	7.4	11.2
Side school	4	426	333	78.17	4.53	4.62	3.2
Episcopal	1	138	95	68.84	1.47	1.32	1.9
U.P.	1	144	110	76.39	1.53	1.53	0.9
Miscellaneous	4	597	495	82.91	6.36	6.86	1.1
Total	103	9403	7212	76.67	100.0	100.0	100.0

Source: PP 1867 xxvi, 212–17.

Table-II: Summary of information on schools in Paisley in 1854

Type of School	No. of schools	No. of students	No. of teachers	No. of students on gratuity	Teacher-student ratio	Percentage of total no. of students
Church of Scotland	19*	1,911	25	213	76.44	37.05
Free Church	4**	351	5	7	70.2	6.81
Episcopal	1	69	1	13	69	1.34
Roman Catholic	1	130	1	70	130	2.52
Private Adv.	25	2,085	34	210	61.32	40.43
Undenominational	2	611	9	210	67.89	11.85
Total	52	5,157	75	513	68.76	100

*The number seems very high; it may be that two or three burgh schools were included in this category.

**Another Free Church school was erected in 1859. Source: PP 1854 / ix, 512.

Table-III: Summary of Information on schools in Greenock in 1854

Type of School	No. of schools	No. of students	No. of teachers	No. of students on gratuity	Teacher-student ratio	Percentage of total no. of students
Church of Scotland	2*	198	2	20	99.0	6.10
Free Church	2	579	7	3	54.14	11.68
Episcopal	3	128	2**	NIL	64.0	3.95
Roman Catholic	2***	250	2	110	125.0	7.71
Private Adv.	11	932	19	401	49.05	28.73

Undenominational	9	1,357	18		75.39	41.83
Total	29	3,244	50	534	64.88	100.0

*Another school under the Church was built in 1859.

**There might be some mistake in the return as the number of teachers was given as two in three schools.

***One more Catholic Church school was erected in the same year.

Source: PP 1854 /ix 512.

Table-IV: Summary of information on schools in Renfrewshire (except Greenock and Paisley in 1865 on area basis)

Name of Parish	Popn.	No. of schools	No. of students on rolls	No. of students present	No. of teachers	Population per school	Teacher-student ratio		Percentage of students on roll present in school
							On roll	Present	
Abbey Paisley	8,412	7	797	607	7+3 PT	1,201.7	130.9	86.7	76.16
Cathcart	3,782	3	313	238	4	1,260.7	78.3	59.5	76.04
Eaglesham	2,328	3	295	240	3	776.0	98.3	80.0	81.36
Eastwood	11,314	15	1,663	1,326	17	754.3	97.8	78.0	79.74
Erskine	1,457	3	201	176	6	485.7	33.5	29.3	87.56
Houston and Killellan	2,470	7	549	395	7	352.9	78.4	56.4	71.95
Inchinnan	619	2	110	110	2	309.5	55.0	55.0	100.0
Inverkip	1,088	2	208	186	2	544.0	104.0	94.0	89.42
Gourock	2,307	2	228	210	2	1,153.5	114.0	105.0	92.11
Kilbarchan	6,348	9	670	478	10+6 PT	709.3	41.9	29.9	71.34

Kilmacolm	1,455	2	162	133	3+1 PT	727.5	40.5	33.3	82.1
Lochwinnoch	3,821	6	561	445	6	636.8	93.5	74.2	79.3
Mearns	3,547	10	599	473	12 +4PT + 1 Asst.	354.7	35.2	27.8	78.96
Neilston	11,013	17	1,142	853	20+2 PT	688.3	51.1	37.4	74.7
Port Glasgow	7,294	10	1,132	716	11	729.4	102.9	65.1	63.25
Renfrew	4,650	5	773	632	11	930.0	70.3	57.5	81.76
Total	71,905	103	9,403	7218	123+ 17PT	698.1	76.45	58.7	76.76
							67.16 (with PT)	51.6 (with PT)	

Source: PP 1867 xxv, 212–17.

Table-V: No. of schools in Abbey Paisley in 1860–61 (other than Johnstone)

Type of Schools	No. of Schools	Children on roll	%
Church of Scotland	3	320	52.0
Subscription	3	190	31.0
Roman Catholic	2	106	17.0
Total	8	616	

Source: PP 1862 xliii. Return of no. of schools in (other than Burgh and adventure schools or schools within a royal burgh) every parish in Scotland, 67.

Endnotes

Chapter 1

1. F. Mort, Renfrewshire (Cambridge, 1912), 4–6.
2. N.S.A., vol–vii (Edinburgh, 1845), 529.
3. J.G. Thomson, 'The County Authority of Renfrewshire', The Educational News, March 14th, 1903, 201.
4. F. Mort, Op. cit., 64–5.
5. Census of Scotland, 1871, vol. II, xl iii.
6. B. Lenman, An Economic History of Modern Scotland 1660–1976, (London, 1977), 105.
7. R. D. Lobban, 'The Migration of the Highlanders into Lowland Scotland (1750– 1890), with particular reference to Greenock', (Unpublished Ph.D. thesis, Edinburgh University, 1969), 25.
8. M. McCarthy, A Social History of Paisley, (Paisley' 1969). p. 103.
9. M. Gray, The Highland Economy 1750–1850, (Oliver and Boyd, 1951). p.255.
10. N. Murray, A Social History of the Scottish Handloom Weavers 1790–1850, (Edinburgh 1976), 65.
11. D. Doherty, The Migration of the highlanders into Lowland Scotland 1780–1850, with particular reference to Paisley; (Honors dissertation, Strathclyde University), 1969. p. 40.
12. R.D. Lobban, op.cit., 41.
13. Address from the Presbytery of Paisley to friends etc., April 1837.
14. Census Enumeration Book, 1851, Milmacolm, 446.
15. M. Gray, op. cit., 255.
16. C.R. Richard, 'Irish Settlement in Nineteenth Century Bradford', Yorkshire Bulletin of Economic and Social Research, 1968 xx 40–57. T. Dillon, 'The Irish in Leeds 1851–61 ', Thorsely Society Publication, LIV pt. I,1-20.

17. J. E. Handley, The Irish in Scotland 1798–1845, (Glasgow, 1945), 49.
18. N. S. A., op. cit., 379–80.
19. M. McCarthy, op. cit., 114.
20. R. Murray Smith, The History of Greenock, (Greenock, 1921), 297.
21. J. E. Handley, op. cit., 51.
22. J. Parkhill, History of Paisley, (Paisley, 1859), 95 and 32.
23. T. S. A., vol. vi. County of Renfrew and Bute, III.
24. H.J. Habakkuk, American and British Technology in the Nineteenth Century, (Cambridge, 1962), 147–50.
25. PP 1839 (159) xiii, Handloom Weavers, Scotland and Continental Europe, pp.11–12.
26. PP 1834 XQ, Select Committee on Handloom Weavers, 958. Quo in Doris D. White, "The Handloom Weavers of Glasgow and Paisley and their relationship with Chartism 1838–42." (unpublished Honours Dissertation, Economic History, Strathclyde University, 1977), 8. And T.C. Smout, "The Strange Intervention of Edward Twistleton: Paisley in Depression, 1841–3," The Search for Wealth and Stability, (London, 1979), 219–20.
27. D. Murray, Reminiscences of Sixty years in the History of Paisley, (Paisley, 1875), 5.
28. R. C. Howard, The Weavers Cottage, Kilbarchan, National Trust Publications, (Edinburgh, 1962), 219.
29. M. Blair, The Paisley Thread Industry, (Paisley, 1907), 183.
30. S. Lythe and J. Butt, An Economic History of Scotland 1100-1939, (Glasgow, 1975), 189. Coats and Cark were owners of the most important thread manufac-tories in the 19th century.
31. H. Hamilton, The Industrial Revolution in Scotland, (Oxford, 1932), 141.
32. T.S.A., op. cit., 379.
33. F. Mort, op. cit., 75.

34. A. Slaven, The Development of the West of Scotland: 1750–1960, (London, 1975), 126–7.
35. R.H. Osborne, 'The Movement of people in Scotland 1851–1951 ', Scottish studies, Vol. II, 1958, 22.
36. Census of Great Britain, 1831, Vol. II.
37. J. Cornwallis Lewis, "The Report of the State of Irish Poor in Great Britain," 1834, 131, quo in M. McCarthy, op. cit., 107.
38. J. E. Handley, op. cit., SO.
39. J. Cornwallis Lewis, op. cit., Evidence of G. Carlyle, a cotton spinner, quo in M. McCarthy, op. cit., 108.
40. J. E. Handley, op. cit., SO. F.D. Macdonald, Scotland's Shifting Population, (Glasgow, 1937), 80.
41. M. McCarthy, op. cit., 98.
42. B.E.A, Collins, op. cit., 154–6, N.S.A., op. cit., 515–24.

Chapter 2

1. M. Monies, "The impact of the 1872 Education (Scotland) Act on Scottish working-class education up to 1899," (Unpublished Ph.D. thesis, University of Edinburgh, 1974), 8–10.
2. A. Bain, education in Stirlingshire (London, 1966), 152.
3. PP 1841 xix, Answer made by schoolmasters in Scotland to queries circulated in 1838, by order of the S.C.E.S. 262–67 and 653–83.
4. T.R. Bone, School Inspection in Scotland I 840–1966, (Edinburgh, 1968), 12.
5. The Times, 18th June, 1939.
6. For a detailed account of the events of Disruption, see R. Buchanon, The Ten Years Conflict, (Glasgow, 1852). 11 vols.
7. J.D. Myers, "Scottish Nationalism and the Antecedents of the 1872 Education Act," Scottish Education Studies, vol. 4, no. 2, Nov., 1972, 74–78.
8. A. Bain, op. cit., I 53.
9. PP 1863 xlvi, Return of amount of subscriptions, donations and collections in places of worship or elsewhere ... 1860–61, House of Commons, 100.

10. E.R.C., General Assembly, 1844, 24.
11. PP 1841 xix, 678.
12. J. Scotland, The History of Scottish Education, vol. I, (London, 1969), 243.
13. PP 1863 xlvi, Return of Amount of Grant paid to each parish or places in 1860–61, 101.
14. David Stow, The training System of Education, Religious, Intellectual and Moral, as established in the Glasgow Normal Training Seminary, (Blackie, 1845), 2–5.
15. IS See Section III, Chapter IV.
16. D. Pride, History of the Parish of Neilston, (Paisley, 1910), 175.
17. See tables I and V in the Appendix.
18. Tables I, II, III and V in the Appendix.
19. PP 1841 xix, 262–683.
20. A. Bain, op. cit., 166–67.
21. PP 1852 iiii, Return Relating to Heritors and Commissioners of Supply, Commission of Supply, 121.
22. N.S.A., op. cit., 166.
23. PP 1863 xlvi, Return of Total Amount of School Salary payable by Landward Heritors, in every parish, under Act 43 Geo 3, c. 54, as at the date of passing of the Act 24 and 25 Vict c 107, 24.
24. D. Pride, op. cit., 173, R. D. Mackenzie, Kilbarchan, A Parish history, (Paisley, 1902), 157.

Chapter 3

1. R. Rait and G.S Pryde, Scotland (London, 1954), 262.
2. A. Allan Maclaren, Religion and Social Class, (London, 1974), 29.
3. PP 1884 xxxii-vi, Report of the commission of the Enquiry on condition of the Crofters and Cottars in the Highlands and Islands.
4. R. Brown, History of Paisley, vol. 11, (Paisley, 1886), 359–62.
5. F. Macarthur, History of Port Glasgow, (Glasgow, 1932), 222.
6. Census of Great Britain, 1851, Religious Education and Workshop, Scotland, Report and Tables.

7. N. L. Walker, Chapter from the history of the Free Church of Scotland, (Edinburgh 1975), 114.
8. A.L. Drummond and J. Bullock, The Church in Victorian Scotland 1843–74, (Edinburgh, 1975), 92.
9. J.G. Paton, Autobiography, (London, 1891), PGAF, Oct., 1843, 81–2.
10. N.L. Walker, op. cit., 94.
11. W. Boyd, Education in Ayrshire through Seven Centuries, 137.
12. Drummond and Bullock, op. cit., 98.
13. See Section I, Chapter v.
14. C.C.M. 1855/6, Cumming, James, Reports on schools Inspected, 596–7.
15. M. Monies, op. cit., 36–7, Section I, Chapter I.
16. Tables I, II and III in the Appendix.
17. PP. 1867 xxv (3858), Appendix to First Report by H.M. Commissioners appointed to Enquire into the Schools of Scotland, 139.
18. Drummond and Bullock, op. cit., 64, (see also II, Chapter I).
19. J. Elder Cumming, The Church of Scotland, Vol VII, (Edinburgh, 1971), 183–4.
20. R. Mitchison, A History of Scotland, (London, 1970), 381.
21. R.M. Smith, op. cit., 269.
22. N.S.A., op.cit.,45, 355.
23. A.C.I., Rigg.
24. Sister Martha Skinnidar, "Catholic Elementary Education in Glasgow 1818–1918," in T.R. Bonn edited, Studies in the History of Scottish Education 1872–1939, (London, 1967), 18.
25. T.R. Bone, op. cit., 54–57.
26. J.E. Handley, op. cit., 302.
27. PP 1867 xxvi, Statistics relative to Schools in Scotland, 212–17.
28. See Table I in the Appendix.
29. PP 1843 xvi, Children's Employment (Traders and Manufacturies), appendix to Second Report, 4.
30. PP 1867 xxvi, 212–17.

31. J. Scotland, op. cit., 256.
32. B.M. Thatcher, "The Episcopal Church in Helensburgh," Scottish Themes, edited by J. Butt and J.T. Ward, (Edinburgh, 1976), I 00.
33. B.M. Thatcher, op. cit., 120.
34. PP 1857/8 xlvi, "Return for the years 1854, 1855 and 1856 restively, of the Names of the Parishes in each county in Scotland in respect of which any money has been paid under the Authority of the Committee of Council on Education," 40, PP 1863, xlvi, 100.)
35. See tables I, II, III and V in the Appendix.

Chapter 4

1. J. Saunders, Scottish Democracy, 1815–40, (Edinburgh, 1950), 265.
2. J. Kerr, Memories Grave and Gay, (Neilson n.d., 1905), 24.
3. T.R. Bone, op. cit., 39.
4. M. Skinnidan, op. cit., 302.
5. T.R. Bone, op. cit., 41
6. PP 1866 xvii (A.C.I) Education (Scotland) Commission, First Report, Minutes of Evidence, 48–9.
7. J. Scotland, op. cit., 71.
8. PP 1867/8 xxix, (A.C. III), Vol. II, Harvey and Cellar, On the State of education in the burgh and Middle Class School, 119–75.
9. J. Clarke, Short Studies in the Education in Scotland, (Edinburgh, 1904), 48.
10. C. Cooper, "The Development of Education in the Burgh of Greenock, with particular reference to the period of First Five Boards 1873–1886," (unpublished M.Ed. thesis, Glasgow University, 1969), 14.
11. PP.1867/8 xxix, Vol. II, 119–121 and 135–37.
12. Anonymous, "Greenock Academy," Scottish County Life, April, 1921, 199.

13. R. Brown, History of Paisley Grammar School, (Paisley, 1875), 128.
14. Ibid., 140.
15. PP xxviii pt. v (3966-v), Schools Inquiry Commission, Hamilton Academy, D.R. Fearon, 1868.
16. C.C.M. 1857/8, J. Gordon, 689.
17. C.C.M. 1856/7, J. Gordon, 636–60.
18. PP 1841 xix, 670–76, PP 1867 xxvi, 217.
19. W.M. Metcalfe, History of Paisley (Paisley, 1909), 349.
20. R. Brown (1886), op. cit., 326, PP 1874 xvii, II Report Endowed Schools and Hospitals (Scotland) Commission, E.S.H.C. 551–9.
21. A.C.I., Gordon.
22. C.C.M. I 850/51, 11, E. Woodford, 736–53.
23. A.C.I., 11.
24. N.S.A., op. cit., 246-8.
25. H.M. Knox, Two Hundred and Fifty Years of Scottish Education 1696–1946, (Oliver and Boyd 1953), 181–2.
26. R. Brown, (1886), op. cit., 331.
27. Ibid., 331, E.A. Clark, 'The Superiority of the Scottish System, Scottish Ragged Schools and their Influence', Scottish Educational Studies, Vol.9. No. 1, May 1977.
28. Ibid., 321.
29. D. Stow, op. cit., 42.
30. C.C.M. 1872/3, D. Middleton, 257.
31. A. Aird, Glimpses of Old Glasgow, (Glasgow 1894), 201.
32. PP 1867/8 xxix, vol I, Burgh and Middle Class schools, 202.
33. J. Knox, 'An Old Educational Reformer', Scottish Educational Journal, No.20, 1953.
34. See Table I, II and III in the Appendix.
35. See Table I in 1. 2.
36. E.G. West, Education and the Industrial Revolution, (London, 1975), 60.
37. PP 1841 xix and see Table XV, 1.3.
38. J. Handly, op. cit., 299.

39. J. Wilson, Tales and Travels of a School Inspector, (Glasgow, 1928), 257.
40. C.C.M. 1843/4, part 11, J. Gibson, 154–66, C.C.M. 1857/8, Gordon, op. cit., 663–93.
41. PP 1841 xix, 653–83.
42. W.M. Metcalfe, op. cit., 394.
43. Table I in the Appendix.
44. See Tables I, II, III and V in the Appendix.
45. See Chapter VI, J. Scotland, op. cit., 195.

Chapter 5

1. C.C.M. 1845, part 11, J. Gordon, 409–24.
2. R.R. Rusk, The training of Teachers in Scotland (Edinburgh, 1928), 94. Church of Scotland's normal school.
3. C.C.M. 1854/5, Woodford, 699–713, C.C.M. 1865/6, Gordon, J. Scotland, op. cit., 319–22.
4. D. Murray, Memories of the Old College of Glasgow, some chapters in the history of the University, (Glasgow, 1927), 559–60.
5. J. Kerr, Scottish Education-School and University from early times to 1908, (Cambridge, 1913), 256.
6. PP 1863 xlvi-100-1 and E.S.H.C. Second Report PP 1886 xxviii.
7. See Tables II, III, IV in the Appendix.
8. E.C.R. 1851, General Assembly of the Church of Scotland.
9. J. Scotland, op. cit., 191.
10. A. Bain, op. cit., 253–4.
11. W. Boyd, op. cit., 133.
12. Free Church Minute 5th vol, 1872.
13. J. C. Jessop, Education in Angus, (Edinburgh 1931), 200.
14. S.S. Lawrie, "Report on Education in the Parochial Schools of the Counties of Aberdeen, Banff and Moray," addressed to the Trustees of the Dick Bequest, Edinburgh 1890, 27–32, J. Scotland, op. cit.
15. See Tables II, III and IV in the Appendix.

16. C.C.M. 1858/9, C.E. Wilson 257–64. H. Mann, 'Report for 1843', Boston, 1865, 393. (195). A.C.I. Gordon, Guthrie.
17. C.C.M. 1866/7, C.E. Wilson, 334-9, A.C.I., S. Laurie.
18. C.C.M. 1871/2, J. Gordon, 82-70, J. Scotland, op. cit., 200.
19. H. Mann, op. cit., 381.
20. PP 1841 xix, 653–83.
21. H. Mann, op. cit., 384.
22. PP 1867 XXV (3845), xliv.
23. R. Brown op. cit., 298.
24. PP 1867/8 xxix, vol. 11, 119–35.
25. PP 1867 xxvi, 213.
26. PP 1867 xxvi, 212–17.
27. R. Brown, (1886), op. cit., 326.
28. PP 1867 xxix, vol. II, 135–751.
29. PP 1867 xxvi, 37-50, 212–17.
30. PP 1867 xxv, (3845) p.xliv.
31. PP 1867/8 xxix, Vol. II, 135–75.
32. PP 1867 xxvi 212–17.
33. N.S.A., Greenock

Chapter 6

1. PP 1839 xiii, F.I.R.
2. B.L. Hutchins and A. Harrison, History of the Factory Legislation, (London, 1903), Chapters YJI-YIII.
3. B. Collins, op. cit., 156–60, N.S.A., op. cit., 19. (219). PP 1843 xvi, Children's Employment, Trade and Manufacture, Appendix to Second Report.
4. PP 1843 xvi, Children's Employment, Trade and Manufacture, Appendix to Second Report, Pt. II, 3–22.
5. PP 1836 xlv, F.I.R., L. Horner, 4, PP 1841 x, F.I.R.
6. PP 1867 XXV (3845 iv) 7–13.
7. N.S.A. 24.
8. PP 1843 xvi, 49.

9. School Board's Second Annual Report, 1875, 188, Census of Scotland 1871, II, cxli.
10. Greenock Advertiser, April 23, 1859, Greenock Town Council Report, July 1, 1862.
11. M. McCarthy, op. cit., 114.
12. PP 1839 (156) xiii, Dr. Austen, Surgeon of Govan reported to the Symon Committee, 19.
13. N. Murray, op. cit., 278, [In rural areas fees in parish schools were 2/6d. a quarter].
14. PP 1864 xxii, Children's Employment, Trade and Manufacture, Second Report With Appendix, 45.
15. N. Murray, op. cit., 275–7.

www.ingramcontent.com/pod-product-compliance
Lightning Source LLC
Chambersburg PA
CBHW071951070426
42453CB00012BA/2103